25

Law in Society Series

In Search of Law

Law in Society Series
EDITED BY C. M. CAMPBELL AND PAUL WILES

Decisions in the Penal Process
A. KEITH BOTTOMLEY

Law and Society: Readings in the Sociology of Law
edited by COLIN CAMPBELL AND PAUL WILES

Deviant Interpretations: Problems in Criminological Theory
edited by DAVID DOWNES AND PAUL ROCK

Female Sexuality and the Law
SUSAN S. M. EDWARDS

The Abuse of Power: Civil Liberties in the United Kingdom
PATRICIA HEWITT

Marx and Engels on Law and Laws
PAUL PHILLIPS

Law in the Balance: Legal Services in the Eighties
edited by PHILIP A. THOMAS

In Search of Law

Sociological Approaches to Law

VILHELM AUBERT

MARTIN ROBERTSON · OXFORD

First published in 1983 by Martin Robertson & Company Ltd.,
108 Cowley Road, Oxford OX4 1JF.

British Library Cataloguing in Publication Data

Aubert, Vilhelm
In search of law. — (Law in society)
1. Sociological jurisprudence
I. Title II. Series
340'.115 K370

ISBN 0-85520-491-5

Typeset by Pioneer, East Sussex
Printed and bound in Great Britain by Billings, Worcester

Contents

Introduction

A profound dualism runs through the legal history as well as the history of legal theory of the Western world. In explicit, theoretical form this dualism is manifest as a contrast between positive and natural law; but it may also seem to ordinary people to be a symptom of the two roles of law: as a coercive force and as a refuge from misery, suppression and injustice. Lon Fuller has characterized the law as a morality of duty, juxtaposed with a morality of aspiration or of excellence.[1] I believe, however, that there is a sense in which law encompasses both duty and the striving towards excellence.

I have not tried to obliterate the dualism inherent in the concept of law. This could be done only by truncating those phenomena that, in one setting or another, are conceived of as law. In the microcosm of these internal tensions between different ideas, one may study, as in a mirror, the clash between forces of greater scope. In this book the dualism is treated as one between law as a technique, guarded by a large and influential professional corps, and law as the expression of human needs, interests and hopes. The latter is no mere chimera; it is increasingly finding expression in constitutions, statutes, treaties and other sources of law. The tension between different concepts of law appears in its most explicit form in debates about human rights. In the last chapter I shall deal with certain aspects of this debate and shall try to show how my preceding analysis may be of relevance to the questions raised by the institutionalization of human rights.

The first two chapters set the scene for what follows through a presentation of certain salient features of the theoretical discussion of the nature of law. Chapter 1 illustrates the variety of attempts to define law, especially the gap between those definitions that are anchored in the supreme force of the state and those that look for a basis beyond the reigning powers. Chapter 2 shows how law, in the sense of the rule of law, was shaped in specific historical circumstances and transformed very largely into a prerogative of the legal profession. Law became a procedural concept, even a question of the techniques of which lawyers, in particular judges, are the masters. It is emphasized, however, that the quest for the rule of law, the public demand, is rooted in deep and pervasive human needs, which can be met only to a limited degree through the methods offered by the legal profession.

The following four chapters deal with positive law, viewed primarily as a technique. Law has many functions, not least as a means of governance, to a large extent through statutory enactments. However, in chapter 3 I try to show how specifically legal techniques, a mode of thinking, of structuring phenomena, have developed as a response to the task of conflict resolution. The structure of this mode of thinking is elaborated in chapters 4 and 5, where legal conceptualizations are confronted with other modes of thinking about social phenomena. Chapter 6 deals largely with law and the discontent it provokes in an attempt to evaluate legal methods from various angles. As mentioned above, the final chapter deals with certain aspects of the human rights problem, linked with a discussion of the new promotional function of legislation.

This book carries the subtitle 'Sociological Approaches to Law'. No more is intended by this than that an essentially interdisciplinary analysis is shaped mainly by the author's primary professional allegiance as a sociologist. This may not be obvious in the two first chapters, which allow philosophers and lawyers to set the stage. The selection of materials, however, is governed by a sociologically founded hypothesis about the functions of law in a field of social conflict. Where a lawyer might strive to find harmony in a system because of his dedication to the task of solving conflicts and contributing to order, a sociologist will probably find it more congenial to describe conflicts and to analyse their implications.

In chapter 3 the sociological perspective is, I believe, transparent. It deals with universals on the micro-sociological level, however, not with macro-sociological explanations for the emergence of particular legal systems. Chapter 4 may appear to contain a logical, rather than a sociological, analysis of legal thinking and decision-making. The aim is not, however, to establish criteria by which to determine whether propositions about law or facts are true, correct or valid; the aim is to analyse legal thinking in terms that are linked to the task of handling conflict and to compare it with other methods that might offer alternative techniques.

In chapter 5 various types of relationships between law and sociology are specified explicitly. In chapter 6 sociology serves in two ways as a means of evaluating law and legal techniques. Based upon empirically established trends in methods of handling conflicts and in the evolution of professional specialties, an attempt is made to use shifts in methods and personnel to evaluate law. The chapter also addresses the consequences of various legal measures and institutions and confronts legal practice with the confessed ideals of legislators or others.

It may be useful to make clear what this book does and does not do, what its (intended and recognized) limitations are. It does not deal with all legal systems of the world. It focuses, with a few exceptions, upon Western law. It is founded upon the author's familiarity with Norwegian law and society. (This is especially true of the materials contained in chapter 6 and of some reflections in chapter 7.) It concentrates upon general problems connected with law. This means, as has already been mentioned, that it is concerned more with forms than with the material content of rules: no systematic attempt has been made to link a specific legal system with a macro-sociological analysis of the social structure of a specific society in a certain period. However, in chapters 2, 5 and 6 it is suggested that the prevalence of legal techniques, as well as the social position of the legal profession, are related to structural features of the society in question.

Notes

1 Lon Fuller, *The Morality of Law* (New Haven/London: Yale University Press, 1964), pp. 5ff.

CHAPTER 1

Concepts of law

The terms 'law', 'justice' and 'right' have as prominent a place in the public consciousness as in the literature of jurisprudence. As basic law words, they are honorific terms; as words that are used colloquially, they are resistant to analytical dissection. They seem to express deeply felt social needs rather than denoting specific and tangible phenomena. If we attempt to define law on this level, we are likely to conclude simply that law is law. That the highest legal authority may find himself in the same position is suggested in Auden's magnificent poem 'Law like Love':

> Law, says the judge as he looks down his nose,
> Speaking clearly and most severely,
> Law is as I've told you before,
> Law is as you know I suppose,
> Law is but let me explain it once more,
> Law is The Law.[1]

However much legal theory and jurisprudence may present definitions of law that relate the term to meticulously specified empirical and normative phenomena, there seems to reside, in the terms themselves, some impregnable emotional nucleus. The basic legal terms 'right', 'law' and 'justice' are loaded and biased in various positive ways. The term 'right' (like *Recht, rett, droit, derecho, diritto*) is connected with the Indo-European root *reg* and the Latin *rectus,* which referred to 'right' (straight) in the physical sense (as opposed to crooked). More interesting, perhaps, is the more recent merger of the legal term 'right' and the term for the right hand. In most (perhaps all) cultures the right side is the good, the clever, the preferred side.[2] Such verbal associations can hardly fail to transfer some emotional significance, even if the semantic meanings are kept firmly separate.

The term 'law' is derived from the Old Norse *log* and the Anglo-Saxon *lagu,* which in turn is thought to have been derived from the verb *leggja,* to lay down or determine. Some linguists have disputed this interpretation, however, and claim a derivation from the Old Norse *lag,* in the sense of team (league).[3] According to this line of reasoning, the origin of the term has to do with a conception of that which binds people together in trade or co-operation. Law is the stuff of which social bonds are made.

More recently, law has also come to be used in referring to the regularities of the natural world, natural laws. It has been claimed by Zilsel and Needham that this terminology was introduced into the natural sciences at the time of the ascendancy of the absolute monarchies and the consolidation of the legal structures of the European states.[4] The link between legal and natural concepts is not of such a recent date, however. The Greek philosophers, among them Plato and Aristotle, used the term *dike* (which has been commonly translated as 'justice') in the context of social as well as natural phenomena.

These various terminological links suggest that it is difficult to change speech habits and semantic meaning simply by analysing legal terms philosophically. A realistic theory of law, as well as a sociology of law, must recognize this fact: these terms fulfil vital ideological functions.

One of the problems that has always faced philosophers and lawyers – and, indeed, everyone who is concerned with law and justice – is the question of whether law belongs to the world of facts or to the world of normative precepts or ideals. What is the relationship between *is* and *ought* in the law? Often this question is dealt with by reference to the distinction between positive and natural law. Adherents of natural law tend not to impeach the value or usefulness of courts or legislative practice as a whole, although they may argue about the ideals that are to be recognized and enforced and may claim greater validity for some norms on the basis of their justification by natural law. There are other thinkers who have maintained that law is a 'negative' phenomenon, not merely because of the inadequacy of the values and ideals that are embedded in any particular legal system but rather because law as such is contrary to basic human interests. This contradiction, it is claimed, can be resolved only through the abolition of law. In the anarchist and Marxist versions of this theory it is especially the governing aspect of law that has stimulated the call for its wholesale rejection as a means of ordering social relations.

The rejection of coercion as a technique of social engineering lies at the root of yet another theory. Here the term 'law' is not debased but reserved as a term of praise, referring to a phenomenon worthy of support and protection. However, the phenomenon is now defined as comprising the informal consensual norms and sentiments of the community and is clearly related to the use of the term 'law' in everyday parlance or in other legal theories. In general, this approach may be viewed as reflecting a preference for extra-legal, rather than legal, modes of ordering social relations and solving problems.

A further contradiction underlying different conceptions of law is one that cannot be expressed by reference to existing schools of legal thought. It springs from conflicting views of man as good or bad, egoistic and competitive or sociable and co-operative, aggressive or loving and charitable. One may trace this contradiction all the way from the conflicts between Aristotelian and Augustinian conceptions of government, through the two versions of social contract theory, the Hobbesian and the Rousseauian, to the sharply contrasting realist theories of Lundstedt and Olivecrona. It is the conception of the *zoon politicon* versus the notion of *homini lupus.* In terms of its consequences for legal policy, this contrast may be more profound than the contradictions between realistic concepts of law and those that are infused with elements of natural law.

Law and coercion

The dilemma inherent in the coercive element of the law is clearly expressed in a report of a conversation about law that is alleged to have taken place 2500 years ago between two famous Athenians, Alcibiades and Pericles, his guardian and head of the government.

'Tell me, Pericles,' [Alcibiades] said, 'could you explain to me what a law is?'

'Why, of course,' said Pericles.

'Then for Heaven's sake explain it,' said Alcibiades, 'for when I hear people praised for being law-abiding I have the idea that a man can't rightly be accorded this praise if he doesn't know what a law is.'

'Well,' said Pericles, 'there is nothing problematical about satisfying your desire to know what a law is. Why, laws are what the people in assembly approve and enact, and they set forth what is or is not to be done.'

'With the idea that good is to be done or bad?'

'By Jove, *good,* my boy, not bad,' said Pericles.

'But if it is not the people who assemble and enact what is or is not to be done but a minority, as in an oligarchy, what are such enactments called?'

'Everything that the sovereign power in the state enacts with due deliberation in determining what is to be done is termed a law,' said Pericles.

'And if a despot with sovereign power in the state enacts rules for the citizens that specify what is to be done, is that also law?'

'Yes,' said Pericles. 'Everything that a despot enacts, as ruler, is termed a law.'

'But, Pericles, force and lawlessness – what are they? Are they not invoked when a stronger man compels a weaker to do his will not by eliciting his consent but by force?'

'That is what I think,' said Pericles.

'Then everything that a despot compels the citizens to do through his enactments without first seeking their consent is lawlessness.'

'That is right,' said Pericles. 'I retract the statement that anything that a despot enacts, as ruler, is law – unless he has secured the consent of the citizens.'

'But the measures that a minority enacts, not with the consent of the majority but through superior power – do we define these as force or not?'

'I think anything that one man compels another to do without his consent, whether by enactment or otherwise, is force rather than consent,' said Pericles.

'Then anything that the whole people enacted without the consent of the well-to-do, because it was stronger than they, would be force rather than law?'

'Alcibiades,' said Pericles, 'let me assure you that when I was your age I too was good at this sort of thing. For we used to practise just the kind of sophistry that I think you are indulging in now.'

And Alcibiades said: 'I should like to have met you in those days, Pericles, when you were at your best.'[5]

The dualism that is inherent in the concept of law is as prevalent in philosophical debates today as it ever was. The tension between justice and power is ineradicable.

In a wide variety of definitions of law some degree of coercion plays a crucial role. A rule that is not in one way or another (directly or indirectly) backed by force is not considered a rule of law. I shall take as a starting-point a rather simple type of definition culled from a basic introductory legal text used in Norway:

That backbone which any society needs to keep itself upright cannot be provided by moral precepts. There is a need for more tangible rules, which are backed by organized power. Such rules are *legal rules*. If a man violates the moral commandment to love his enemies, this will entail no external consequences. If he steals a piece of ham, however, he will be arrested and punished, and if he does not, of his own free will, leave a farm that he has forfeited, the bailiff will throw him out.[6]

A popular English introductory text makes a similar point:

Many legal writers deprecate the emphasis upon the ultimate sanction of force in the definition of law. Thus Professor Goodhart has recently emphasized that the motives for obedience are many . . .

Whatever may be said of motives for obedience to law, therefore, it is only by the application of some sanction that such obedience is secured where it really matters.[7]

These observations contain the seeds of a theory about how people behave in relation to legal rules and why they do so. Both have a place within a long European tradition of positivism in legal thought. This tradition merits serious attention, but it is hardly fruitful to try to classify legal theorists either as positivists or as adherents of natural law. We should, rather, look upon the positivist element as an ingredient of almost all legal theories, a theme that may be more or less dominant.

An early forerunner of the positivist definition of law is to be found in the work of the late medieval scholar Marsilius of Padua (1275–1342). According to Marsilius, law may be considered in two ways:

In one way in itself, insofar as it *only shows* what is just or unjust, beneficial or harmful, and as such it is called the science or doctrine of right. In another way it may be considered according to whether observance to it is sanctioned by a command and is distributed in the present world; *and considered in this way it most properly is called, and is, law.* (Translator's emphasis)[8]

Machiavelli carried on the tradition from Marsilius. He was not concerned with drawing lines between legal rules and other instruments of princely governance and put the emphasis very firmly upon the military aspect of power. He was, however, concerned with questions of legitimacy; and any theory of state power is also of implicit relevance to legal theory. In one of his explicit references to law Machiavelli came close to giving a positivist definition of the validity of law:

> As there cannot be good laws where the state is not well armed, it follows that where they are all armed they have good laws. I shall leave the laws out of the discussion and speak of the arms.[9]

Among jurists John Austin is considered the founding father of 'analytical legal positivism'. He conceived of law as commands backed by force: 'Austin's most important contribution to legal theory was his substitution of the command of the sovereign (i.e. the state) for any ideal of justice in the definition of law.'[10] The definition of the sovereign is linked to 'habitual obedience from the bulk of a given society'. Thus even within the framework of this theory there might be room for the concept of an usurper, a power-holder without legitimacy. However, the main thrust of Austin's argument is to associate law intimately with power and coercion. 'Every sanction properly so called is an eventual evil annexed to a command.'[11]

The leading German legal theorists of the second half of the last century, von Ihering and Georg Jellinek, also defined law by reference to the force of the state: 'The coercion of the state constitutes the absolute criterion of the law. A legal norm without legal coercion is in itself a contradiction in terms, a fire that does not burn, a light that does not illuminate.'[12] However, Ihering's emphasis upon force was tempered by his linking of law, almost by definition, to interests, values and utility.[13] A somewhat less illustrious scholar, Rudolph Sohm, gave vent to a more Teutonic expression of this philosophy in a much read textbook:

> Law is the organization of the people *in their struggle for life.* Therefore, war is the father (begetter) of law. 'War is the father of all things.' Under the threat of impending war the people join forces in the army and the state. War is not socially destructive but socially constructive violence. The order of the army is at the root of the legal order: the soldier is the father of the fatherland. The constitution of the army calls forth the constitution of the state, and the distribution of war booty produces the property. Under the sign of the spear (*sub hasta*) are the law and the state born. (Original emphasis)[14]

Among modern philosophers of law H. L. A. Hart is one of the most subtle and sophisticated proponents of a positivist view of law. He deviates from his predecessor Austin, however, in his emphasis upon the set of secondary rules, the rules of recognition that form the foundation of the authority of those who make the laws. In a limited sense, this draws the legal consciousness of the citizens within the definition of the law.[15] Yet the two most important schools of thought of this century that have furthered the positivist cause are the Scandinavian school of legal realism (the Uppsala philosophy) and the American legal realists. There are many differences between the two schools and between the individual scholars within each of them. In what follows scant justice is done to the full complexity and sophistication of the analyses of these legal theoreticians.

Scandinavian legal realism

The point of departure for the Uppsala philosophers is far removed from the realities and dictates of the law. It is to be found in their conception of philosophy as logical analysis, which they shared with the logical empiricists of the Vienna circle in the period between the two World Wars and the Cambridge philosophers led by G. H. Moore. Starting from the rejection of metaphysics, Axel Hägerström and, later, Anders Vilhelm Lundstedt built an epistemological theory of law and morals that has been termed 'value nihilism' (*värdenihilismen*).[16] This, the main thesis of the Uppsala philosophy, denies that normative sentences such as 'This is right', 'This is good', 'This ought to be done' can be true or false. Such sentences lack logical meaning and have no factual content, no bearing upon reality. And since the task of science is to produce true propositions and hypotheses, there is no room for such normative sentences in science.

From these premises Hägerström and Lundstedt drew the conclusion that existing legal scholarship that made use of normative formulations was metaphysical and unscientific and did not deal with facts in the world of reality. This led to the awkward consequence that legal rules, rights and obligations, the legal order and the state, did not exist. In order to avoid this unacceptable conclusion, Hägerström and Lundstedt proposed that statements about valid law (*gällande rätt*), in spite of their lack of logical meaning, had a foundation in fact: the observable regularities of the behaviour of public authorities, the sanctions imposed on those who do not comply with the law. Thus, starting from a certain conception of the nature of philosophy and of science,

Hägerström and Lundstedt arrived at a legal theory according to which the threat of coercion seemed to be the driving force behind legal institutions.

The dualism and ambivalence of this theory have been criticized by Ingemar Hedenius. He maintains that a non-metaphysical, empirical meaning can be attributed to sentences about valid law when they occur within the framework of legal scholarship. He states that 'the validity of a rule means that it is in fact enforced':

> A valid rule of law can be nothing but a rule of behaviour that is actually being enforced, a habit that, by and large, is being exercised by certain persons in authority.[17]

He makes this point more precisely when he writes:

> That something is contrary to law, that a right or an obligation exists, is synonymous with claiming that certain rules of law have validity with respect to specific cases. That a rule of law is valid means that it is a rule of behaviour that is actually being applied by certain persons in authority, appointed for this purpose. Thus, the validity of a specific rule of law is synonymous with the existence of an empirical regularity in human behaviour. This is always a question of behaviour on the part of legal authorities. Regularities in the behaviour of other persons, or of legal authorities outside their field of public authority, cannot acquire the status of a legal rule.[18]

Hedenius makes it quite clear that the term 'valid law' refers to purely empirical phenomena, that these have to do with the behaviour of agents of public authority and that these public agencies are authorized to apply force to achieve compliance with their decisions.[19]

Among the Uppsala philosophers, Karl Olivecrona has placed the greatest emphasis on coercion, but he locates it elsewhere. He views the law as a system within which there are many rules that lack separate backing in force (for example, in civil and constitutional law). He even maintains that 'In the very centre of the legal system sanctions lose their significance.'[20] However, all legal rules function within the systemic framework of a state that possesses a monopoly in the use of organized, coercive military power. It is the police and the military that distinguish the state from other types of organization. After having mentioned the diverse positive functions of a welfare state, Olivecrona claims that 'all this presupposes the organization of the physical means of coercion and cannot prevail without these. In the final analysis it rests upon the monopolization of the weapon force. It forms the nucleus of the state organization.'[21]

The Scandinavian philosopher of law who has offered the most penetrating and sophisticated theory of valid law, anchored in purely empirical phenomena, is Alf Ross, who defines legal philosophy as a discipline aiming at a study of legal scholarship. The problem of the nature of law, when the metaphysical aspect is discarded, is the problem of interpreting the concept of 'valid law' as an integral part of doctrinal legal sentences. Like the Uppsala philosophers, Ross defines law by reference to the activities of persons in authority, the judiciary:

> A national law system, considered as a valid system of norms, can accordingly be defined as the norms which actually are operative in the mind of the judge because they are felt by him to be socially binding and therefore obeyed. The test of the validity is that on this hypothesis – that is, accepting the system of norms as a scheme of interpretation – we can comprehend the actions of the judge (the decisions of the courts) as meaningful responses to given conditions and within certain limits predict them – in the same way as the norms of chess enable us to understand the moves of the players as meaningful responses and predict them.[22]

He emphasizes that the judge is the central figure in this theory:

> Only the legal phenomena in the narrower sense, however – the application of the law by the courts – are decisive in determining the validity of the legal norm. In contrast to generally accepted ideas, it must be emphasized that the law provides the norms for the behaviour of the courts and not of private individuals. The effectiveness which conditions the validity of the norms can therefore be sought solely in the judicial application of the law and not in the law in action among private individuals. If, for example, criminal abortion is prohibited, the true content of the law consists in a directive to the judge that he shall under certain conditions impose a penalty for criminal abortion. The decisive factor determining that the prohibition is valid law is solely the fact that it is effectively upheld by the courts where breaches of the law are brought to light and prosecuted. It makes no difference whether the people comply with or frequently ignore the prohibition. This indifference results in the apparent paradox that the more effectively a rule is complied with in extra-judicial life, the more difficult it is to ascertain whether the rule possesses validity, because the courts have that much less opportunity to manifest their reaction.[23]

Ross links law with force according to this formulation: 'A national law system is the rules for the establishment and functioning of the state machinery of force.'[24]

Unlike the American legal realists and earlier representatives of legal positivism, the Uppsala philosophers, Lundstedt, Olivecrona and Ekelöf, developed theories about the factual operation of the threat of coercion. They wrote extensively, albeit on a speculative basis, about the deterrent (moral-building) impact of punishment. (It ought to be mentioned here that many adherents of a theory of natural law, like Grotius and Blackstone, also emphasize the deterrent purpose and effect of penalties – one sign that the lines of distinction between schools of thought are blurred and that the rigid classification of thinkers may often be misleading.) All three authors share a strong belief in the potential of the penal system for influencing people, which is a principal theme in their theories about the nature of law; but they differ considerably with respect to the mode of operation of penalties and the psychological assumptions underlying the hypotheses advanced.

Lundstedt's theory is the 'softest'. He does not have much faith in straightforward deterrence based upon the naked threat of force. Penalties must somehow appeal to the moral consciousness of the public in order to function effectively. Laws without the support of current mores run the risk of being ineffectual or, at worst, of undermining public confidence in the legal system. Thus, in principle, Lundstedt is not far removed from Sumner, although his view of legislation is much more positive than Sumner's. Lundstedt was a social democrat.[25]

Ekelöf concurs with Lundstedt in so far as he also emphasizes the importance of building a morality, not merely compliance out of fear of sanctions, although he attributes greater weight to deterrence than does his older colleague. Indignation at those who violate the law mediates the moral influence exerted through penalties. Ekelöf puts the greater emphasis upon the habit-forming influence of sanctions, which eliminates the need for reflection, and on conscious choice of a compliant course of action.[26]

Olivecrona is in some respects the hawk among the Uppsala philosophers, presenting an image of man and society that is sometimes reminiscent of Hobbes's *Homo homini lupus.* He believes more firmly in naked deterrence than do his two colleagues. To him an important psychological mechanism consists in the avoidance of internal conflict that might arise as a consequence of the suppression of any thought of delinquency when under the threat of sanctions.[27, 28]

American legal realism

It would be neither possible nor useful in this context to attempt a detailed presentation of American legal realism. This has been done elsewhere.[29] However, American legal realism must be mentioned because one of its facets is an emphasis upon law as fact, as a phenomenon that is, in the eyes of many legal realists, amenable to study by the methods of social science.

Much has been made of the definitions of law presented by American realists, some of which are strongly reminiscent of those offered at about the same time by the Scandinavian realists. Many followed up O. W. Holme's dictum about law's being what the courts do in fact. John Chipman Gray maintained:

> The Law of the State or of any organized body of men is composed of the rules which the courts, that is, the judicial organs of that body, lay down for the determination of legal rights and duties.[30]

Cook phrased it thus:

> Lawyers, like the physical scientists, are engaged in the study of objective physical phenomena . . . As lawyers we are interested in knowing how certain officials of society . . . have behaved in the past in order that we may make a prediction of their probable behaviour in the future.[31]

And Karl Llewellyn, considered by many to be the most important figure in the realist movement, also made statements that were similar to those of the Uppsala philosophers:

> This doing of something about disputes, this doing of it reasonably, is the business of law. And the people who have the doing in charge, whether they be judges or sheriffs or clerks or jailers or lawyers, are officials of the law. What these officials do about disputes is, to my mind, the law itself.[32]

In many ways, however, the similarities between the American and the Scandinavian legal realists are superficial; and the 'flavour' of their writings differs. The styles of Llewellyn and Lundstedt, both of them professors of law, do not have much in common. Yet the emphasis upon the scientific character of the study of law is a point of convergence. Some of the American realists drew from this fact the conclusion that there was a need for innovative studies based on new empirical methods.[33] In the cases of Llewellyn and Underhill Moore, it led them far into the fields of the social sciences, social anthropology and cognitive psychology.[34] The

Uppsala philosophers (and Ross), on the other hand, did not see any need to revise the methods of legal scholarship. They, and specially Lundstedt, seem to have believed that they could transform law into a science through the systematic redefinition of the basic, previously metaphysical, terms.

This may reflect another difference, which has to do with their relationship with philosophy: 'One of the safer generalizations that can be made about realists from Corbin (or Gray) to Llewellyn or Douglas or Moore is that they did not look upon themselves as philosophers.'[35] Hägerstrøm, by contrast, was a philosopher, as were and are several others of the Uppsala school. In general, Scandinavian legal realism has been closely associated with philosophy.

It may be more than an accident that several of the leading American realists (Corbin, Hohfeld, Cook) had some background in the natural sciences, and Llewellyn, as a student at Yale, was strongly influenced by the sociologist William Graham Summer.[36] Hägerstrøm, on the other hand, began his career as a student of divinity.

The American legal realists were much preoccupied by the problems of, and attempts to reform, legal education. They were also concerned about the lack of uniformity in American law, based upon the federal state system. Parallel concerns have played no important role within the Scandinavian school.

Holmes's approach to law from 'the bad man's point of view' is symptomatic of another characteristic of the American as compared with the Scandinavian realists. The Americans view law largely from the point of view of the practising lawyer, the advocate, the defendant or, even more, the parties in civil litigation. The improvement of legal craftmanship is central to that movement. The Scandinavian realists have tended to look upon law more from the point of view of the legislator and the planner and have given some consideration to social survival. This emerges most clearly from their discussions of general deterrence, discussions that sometimes have a distinctly authoritarian and paternalistic tinge.

The relationship between legal realism and the emerging sociology of law is problematic both in the United States and in Scandinavia.[37] It would seem that the realists had a stronger direct influence on Scandinavian sociologists of law than on those in the

United States – in spite of the fact that American realists were oriented more towards social science than were their Scandinavian counterparts. Most of the first generation of legal sociologists in Scandinavia were trained as lawyers and were naturally schooled early in contemporary legal theory. American sociology of law, however, has drawn its recruits to a larger extent from sociology or social anthropology. It is difficult to discern any direct link between the realists and the present legal sociologists.

Natural law

The positivist or realist schools of legal philosophy are of particular interest because they insist that law is an empirical phenomenon – it comprises facts, and facts that are related to coercion. In the introductory paragraphs of this chapter it was emphasized that the basic terms of law have honorific meanings that refer to an unspecified and somewhat diffuse 'goodness'. This quality of the law has been elaborated and developed into grand theories linked with some conception of natural law.[38]

From ancient times there has been the notion that a law exists that is above men – not merely above the ordinary citizen, but also above those in power, even the sovereign. The norms that have this character have been called 'natural law'. We find the contrast between these norms and the positive commands issued by those in power in the Greek tragedies.

In its ancient form natural law was of religious origin. God and the Ten Commandments were sources of Christian law. The law of Islam and Judaism fuses the sacred and the profane even to this day. In Roman law *ius naturale* played an important part. This concept, however, was rooted in typically mundane interests, tied to the efforts to build, and preserve the unity of, an empire that was composed of a variety of peoples and cultures, each with its own legal tradition, and that was threatened constantly by rebellion at its centre and erosion on the periphery.

Throughout the Middle Ages in Europe ideas of natural law served primarily the interests of the Church and the Papacy. Natural and Roman law were integrating factors in medieval European culture, common elements that crossed the borders between local communities and the barriers of language, transcended local customs and local legal traditions. As long as it was in the hands of the Papacy, however, natural law was an impediment to the growth of nation states, though both Marsilius of Padua and Machiavelli made attempts to secularize the law and became, as we have seen, forerunners of legal positivism.

Natural law survived these attacks and was presented eventually in a new, secular guise by the Dutchman Hugo Grotius,[39] who wrote under the influence of geographical discoveries, of expanding commerce and sea transport accompanied by risks of piracy. The world was being drawn together anew, once again approaching the unity that it had seemed to possess in Roman times. Principles of coexistence were needed in a world in which there existed no superior power able to sanction breaches of such rules. The source of law could not be anchored in a sovereign; it had to be located elsewhere. Grotius sought to found it in human reason. It may be noted that the problem still exists today; human reason has not as yet been victorious in its efforts to settle international conflicts.

Within the framework of natural law two conceptions were to play a dominant part in European political development: the idea of the social contract and the notion of inherent human rights. The idea of the social contract, the notion that we must conceive of society (that is to say, the nation state) as founded upon a covenant, a pact between the citizens, constitutes the foundation of later theories of democracy, representative government and the sovereignty of the people. In the version of Thomas Hobbes the theory of the social contract, in accordance with the tradition of Augustine, was built upon an image of man as wicked, sinful and aggressive, while also possessing a peculiarly rational disposition. In their own selfish interests men had to join together in a common endeavour to limit strife and the disasters of a war of all against all. This could best be achieved by an agreement to cede the right of decision-making to a superior power, provided with the necessary means to prevent civil war. In Rousseau's version the theory of the social contract was built, in accordance with Aristotle's conception of man as a *zoon politicon,* upon the notion that man is, by nature, able to live in harmony with his fellow men.

The theory of inherent human rights – to life, liberty and property – as espoused by Locke and Rousseau, was given public sanction in the French Declaration of Human Rights of 1789 and in the American Declaration of Independence of 1776. We find in these declarations an ideological basis for the defence of the individual and of the rule of law in the relationship between the minority and the dominant majority.

The revival of natural law

It is a widespread notion that the post-war period has seen a revival or renaissance of natural law theory. A particularly clear formulation of this new stance is to be found in papers published by the old and respected German jurist Gustav Radbruch, in the years immediately after the fall of the Nazi regime, which made explicit reference to the fearful consequences of a positivist approach when an evil government issues inhuman laws. He felt that in such circumstances one had to reject the thesis *Gesetz ist Gesetz* (law is law).[40] I can myself remember my professor, Frede Castberg, warning me as a student, during the German occupation of Norway, that my positivist views could in theory – practice was different – lead to the unwitting acceptance of Nazi ordinances as law.

The impact of the Hitler period, and of the Nuremberg trials, upon post-war German philosophy of law must have been profound. In a series of papers, collected under the title *Natural Law or Legal Positivism,*[41] a number of eminent jurists testify to renewed interest in doctrines of natural law. This is not the place to provide a detailed logical analysis of these doctrines; it is anyway in their nature to defy conclusive logical analysis. What is important is their expression of unease about positivist doctrines of law, their quest for a point of observation and action beyond existing positive law and their unwillingness to characterize this as something extra-legal, unworthy of the designation 'law' in the honorific sense.

We shall, in the last chapter of this book, have occasion to discuss more fully the meaning of 'law' when the term is used in the context of phenomena that transcend the rules that are enforced by governmental machinery. This will be done, however, not with reference to the revival of natural law among philosophers of law but through a review of debates and declarations, in national and international political fora, about human rights. This seems to be a more important trend, and it is one that may be viewed as an outgrowth of the natural law doctrines of the Enlightenment.

However, even the somewhat esoteric debates among philosophers and legal theorists are symptomatic of wider currents in the world community. And it would be a mistake to focus exclusively on the formative influence of Hitler's tyranny. The papers of the World Congress on Philosophy of Law and Social Philosophy held in St Louis in 1975 were collected in three volumes under the title *Equality and Freedom.*[42] It is not only the title that evokes associations with the natural law ideals of the American and French revolutions; numerous contributions also testify to the great efforts to transcend, in theory at least, the limitations that the positive laws of countries in various parts of the world impose on attempts to realize equality and freedom. These efforts are not, on the whole, cloaked in the old language of natural law theory. However, the idealist and reformist nature of the contributions parallel those of progressive natural law doctrines of the past. And it is remarkable how few traces can be found of the intricate, detailed, often very sophisticated logical and conceptual analyses that used to characterize discussions in positivist schools of jurisprudence. There runs through a large number of the papers a desire to find some kind of legal support and basis for social arrangements that have not as yet come under the regulation of positive, enforced law.

Furthermore, among philosophers and jurists dedicated to the rigours of logical analysis and respect for empirical data, there is emerging a new orientation and a willingness to deal with concepts that in a more dogmatic, positivist era were rejected as metaphysical. Within Scandinavian legal theory one can perceive a great difference between Alf Ross and Torstein Eckhoff in their approaches to the concept of justice. Ross claims that 'as characterizations of a rule or order, the words "just" and "unjust" are entirely devoid of meaning . . . In this context the words have no descriptive meaning at all.'[43] And he goes on to maintain that an appeal to justice is an emotional attempt to truncate rational argument that might lead to a better understanding.[44] Although there are more nuances in Ross's attitude to justice,[45] his treatment smacks of hostility to the term itself. Eckhoff's approach is different, terminologically speaking. He believes that questions of justice are very important. However, he approaches the problem from a methodological perspective related to logical positivism, presenting himself as an observer of debates about justice, not a participant.[46] Thus, it would be a mistake, even an injustice, to classify Eckhoff's work as an off-shoot of natural law doctrines. But it represents an important deviation from the narrow path of Scandinavian legal realism. Although he claims to be merely an observer, Eckhoff has prepared the ground for those who want to participate, through argument, in the search for ideals of justice.

If we want to find a philosopher who participates in the debate about justice, it is natural to point to John Rawls and his influential (or, at least, much discussed) *A Theory of Justice.* Here we find distinct echoes of elements of past doctrines of natural law. The relationship is evident in Rawls's blunt statement: 'Justice is the first virtue of social institutions as truth is of systems of thought.'[47] Like Hobbes and Rousseau, Rawls bases his argument upon a model situation in which a social contract is assumed: 'In justice as fairness the original position of equality corresponds to the state of nature in the traditional theory of the social contract.'[48]

The affinity to natural law theories, not least the revived version of the post-Nazi philosophers and jurists, is most clearly demonstrated in Rawls' treatment of the problems posed by civil disobedience, the right to resist the enforcement of positive law. Rawls believes that such a right exists and should be exercised in certain carefully circumscribed situations. Many so-called positivists would agree with this, maintaining that morality may sometimes take precedence over law. However, Rawls seeks a basis for resistance not in morals but in principles of a different order, namely, principles of justice:

> To act autonomously and responsibly a citizen must look to the political principles that underlie and guide the interpretation of the constitution. He must try to assess how these principles should be applied in the existing circumstances. If he comes to the conclusion after due consideration that civil disobedience is justified and conducts himself accordingly, he acts conscientiously.[49]

The normative basis for action consists in a blend of subjective conviction and reference to collectively accepted principles, more or less embedded in, or assumed by, positive law. Unlike the traditional adherents of a natural law doctrine, Rawls does not believe that there exists a final, authoritative arbiter in questions concerning the interpretation of the 'constitution'. But, in conformity with the natural law tradition, he seems to believe in the existence of principles of a higher order, enabling citizens to assess, and conceivably reject, a legislator's commands.

We may look upon modern versions of natural law doctrine as but one group within a wider class of theories that deviate from legal realism. The one element that all these theories have in common is that they provide a point of observation or evaluation from which positive law may be criticized. The theories range from the wholesale rejection of law as a bourgeois phenomenon, as in classical Marxist theories of law and state, to the democratic notion that law is to be found in the legal consciousness of the people. It may even be claimed that contemporary sociology of law (otherwise rather different) shares with such theories a concern to provide the basis of a critical stance *vis-à-vis* prevailing legal principles.

Viewed from this perspective, the sociology of law is a critical science but not a visionary one. Within dominant schools of sociological thought there is hardly a basis for the framing of new legal rules or doctrines to supplant the prevailing ones. Social research may, by virtue of its critical potential, suggest ideals that deviate from positive law or fill lacunae in the established system. However, the establishment of alternative rules or decisions falls outside the scope of the social sciences as they are conventionally understood.

The classical Marxist approach to law, with its denial of the validity of bourgeois law, has created the possibility of the establishment of new legal doctrines and the promulgation of much new and original legislation. After a phase of revolutionary reforms, however, Soviet law and related legal systems have apparently returned to positivism. Yet it remains a characteristic of communist legal doctrine that an overriding ideology, which is written into the constitution, serves to guide legal interpretation. To the extent that this allows for deviation from positive law, it differs from other doctrines in that it is the political leadership itself that may 'utilize' the leeway.

The legal doctrines of communist states, with their constitutional references to the working class, are in principle no different from legal theories that attempt to anchor the validity of the law in the legal consciousness of the people. Since the exact nature and distribution of attitudes to the law are largely unknown, this principle provides the proponents of the doctrine with considerable freedom to amend or modify positive law in accordance with the normative principles to which they themselves subscribe. Quite another matter is whether such arguments will be effective in encounters with the authorities – legislative, judicial or administrative – that subscribe to a positivist doctrine or have different conceptions of the legal consciousness of the people.

The general legal consciousness

Austin located the criteria of legal validity in the decisions made by the authorities. So too, in a different way, did the American and Scandinavian legal realists. The adherents of natural law anchored its validity in a source above the government. There is a school of legal theory, however, whose adherents have tried to found the validity of law on a source *below* the government; they have located it in the grass roots and make the claim that valid legal rules must correspond to, or be derived from, the legal consciousness of the people. This point of view became a part of the jurisprudential tradition through the historical school, first and most prominently in the work of the German Savigny.[50] Subsequently, other scholars have maintained similar views with rather more consistency. Savigny became, in practice, a spokesman for the absorption of classical Roman law, which could hardly be said to represent popular customs and attitudes.

In an overview of the different schools of legal sociology the famous American lawyer Roscoe Pound suggested that sociologists tend to use a very broad definition of law. He claimed that they have tended to use it as though it was more or less identical with social norms and social control generally.[51] This implies that the law is to be found in the attitudes and interaction of people, without much reference to legislation or judicial precedents. Pound's characterization may have some validity in relation to the sociological 'classics'. In modern sociology, however, one rarely, if ever, encounters such an expansive definition of law.

Among the more 'classical' sociological theories of law there are conservative as well as radical versions. The ideological function of a reference to legal consciousness is ambiguous. An attempt to root the law in the common legal consciousness may be seen as an expression of a populistic or democratic ideology. We shall soon see some examples of this. There is also, however, a conservative version, which may be detected in the works of Comte,[52] Spencer[53] and Sumner.[54] These social theorists emphasized the social processes in society and the spontaneous forces and attitudes that operate in this context. At the same time they opposed efforts to change society through legislation. They considered such a policy futile and thus became defenders of the *status quo,* by contrast with Marxist legal theorists who shared a sceptical attitude to legislation as a means of changing society and opted for revolution instead.

It is perhaps no accident that some of the best-known theories of law as a phenomenon located in the attitudes and behaviour of people had their origin in Tsarist Russia and the tottering Austro-Hungarian Empire. The Pole Petrazycki,[55] the Russian Sorokin[56] and the Austrian Ehrlich[57] presented theories of a law that resides in mundane social interaction and in local communities. Social control through law is built into, and is inseparable from, personal contacts between people. The historical background for these theories was states in which a great distance separated the commands of the legislator from local customs and norms, and where the legitimacy of the government was questionable. Suppressed national minorities strongly resented and resisted the policy of the central government.[58]

Within Scandinavian legal realism one can also find definitions of law rooted in the general legal consciousness. In Alf Ross's earlier work the claim is made that a rule with which people comply can be termed a rule of law only if compliance is motivated by something other than fear of sanctions. There has to exist the moral conviction that a rule is legal. A commentator on Ross's philosophy of law points to the correspondence between this kind of definition and democratic ideology.[59] In his later work, as mentioned above, Ross has developed another concept of law that places emphasis on the ideology of the judge and not on the general legal consciousness.

A colleague of Ross, Illum, maintained in 1945, the year of Denmark's liberation from German occupation, that it is not a sufficient condition for the emergence of a legal rule that it has been promulgated by the state according to proper procedures. It becomes law only if, in addition, it becomes a part of the common legal consciousness. He pursued this line of thinking and concluded with the following rather unconventional view: 'One seeks the law, only to find individual conceptions of law held by particular people. The law exists in as many variations as there exist individual conceptions of the law.'[60]

One should not be misled into drawing political conclusions from such definitions, which anchor law in the attitudes of the people. In principle, this can appear to be a kind of ideological short-cut to democratic control. In practice, however, reliance on the consciousness of the people or of the working class can turn into a dangerous weapon in the hands of an unscrupulous government. It violates the rule of law and the requirement for precise rules defining the relationship between the individual and the government, rules that are upheld through the supervision of an independent judiciary. Arbitrary decisions can be made under a cloak of references to the will of the people unless this will is harnessed to rules that constrain the government in very precise terms.

The Marxist theory of law

The schools that embrace the theory of law dealt with above all present 'law' as an honorific term. Law is regarded as something good and necessary. There is, however, an important and influential school of thought by which law is considered neither valuable nor necessary; it is, rather, associated with particular epochs in the evolution of societies. Law has to be superseded by other types of social mechanism. The future society, the ideal society, will be one that has been liberated from legal control, one in which law has been replaced by other mechanisms of governance and conflict resolution.

A number of communists and anarchists, such as Godwin, Proudhon, Stirner, Bakunin and Krapotkin, have adopted such a view of the law. However, by far the most influential of the theories that depict law as a negative phenomenon is the one espoused by Marx, Engels, Lenin, Pashukanis and others. In the eyes of Marx and Engels, law was a bourgeois phenomenon, linked with the capitalist mode of production, which it mirrored. Law was a superstructure built on a base of specific material conditions, commodity production and market relations in a capitalist society. As an aspect of the state, law was a means of suppression, organized power in the hands of the capitalists that was directed against the proletariat. Both state and law had their origins in the insoluble contradictions that divide the social classes under capitalism.[61]

A revolutionary change in the relations of production and between the classes would not lead simply to a new legal system; it would lead to the withering away of the state and the total disappearance of law. However, this state of affairs would not emerge until communism was established. During an intermediary phase, under socialism and the dictatorship of the proletariat, state and law would still persist because the contradiction between the classes would not have subsided and commodity exchange would still take place: the 'realm of necessity' would still not have been replaced by the 'realm of freedom'. Lenin developed the theory of the dictatorship of the proletariat and of state and law as means of governance during the period of transition from socialism to communism. Lenin, however, upheld the view of Marx and Engels that state and law would disappear under communism. It would not be abolished by decree. It would simply wither away as a consequence of the changes taking place in the material base of society. However, he took the precaution of pointing out that this process might take a long time.[62]

With the benefit of hindsight, one might ask whether this was mere word play, a shift of terminology, rather than a theory of transition to something qualitatively different from what other theorists have called law. What was thought to be the substitute for law in the communist society? Marx seems to have thought that spontaneous group processes between free individuals who did not exploit each other would solve problems and conflicts through a form of self-regulation. He may have had in mind modes of conflict resolution found in certain so-called primitive societies and in some rural communities.

An important notion in the writings of Marx and Engels was that the relationships of domination between people would be replaced by the administration of things. With the growth of the complexity of the socio-economic system, it would become increasingly Utopian to rely on purely spontaneous social control. Planning would be essential even under communism. Alongside the spontaneous and free group processes, the Plan emerges as a substitute for the law. This contrast between the law and the Plan has been elaborated upon above all by Pashukanis.[63]

Because of the development of modern administrative law in the service of economic and social planning in the most advanced capitalist countries, the term 'plan' evokes an image of something legal. Pashukanis, however, chose such a restrictive definition of the concept of law that it could not cover an administrative system of rules. It may seem as if this definition was chosen because of a wish to retain the Leninist theory of the withering away of state and law while avoiding the trap of wishful thinking about the spontaneous co-ordination of an advanced economy.

The very essence of law, according to Pashukanis, is the notion of one legal subject facing another on the basis of assumed equality or parity. Legal relations typically provide a basis for litigation and not for decisions by acts of the administration. Contract is the pivotal legal concept, as opposed to the decree or the command. Legal concepts and principles presuppose that every legal subject has individuality and acts freely in relation to every other free legal subject, each of them provided with rights and obligations.

The legal subject is, as it were, torn out of his social context and transformed into an abstract category (or role) as buyer, seller, creditor, debtor, mortgagee, etc. The state itself may be involved in relationships of rights and obligations with its citizens. Legal suits may occur between citizens and the state, based upon a notion of formal parity. According to Pashukanis, the law of contract sets the pattern for all fields of bourgeois law, including administrative law, family law and criminal law. However, the formal equality between the parties to the contract masks a profound and real inequality and injustice. The 'republic of the market' hides the 'despotism of the factory'.

Contrary to earlier Marxist thinkers, Pashukanis did not consider the element of force and coercion a sufficient criterion in the definition of law. The backing of the coercive power of the state was a necessary criterion but not a sufficient one to provide a rule with legal character. Instructions and decrees within the Army or the Church could be underpinned by the coercive power of the state without being rules of law. Such rules are based upon an hierarchical system of subordination, presupposing obedience to commands and not a definition of rights.

Pashukanis' analysis of law as a bourgeois phenomenon was in conflict with Stalin's policy in the late 1930s. He was condemned as a traitor and disappeared without trace in 1937. In opposition to him stood the theory of socialism in one country, surrounded by dangerous enemies, demanding the strengthening of state power, not its withering away. In the Soviet Union the state was built on legal forms, law books, legal scholarship, trained lawyers and most of the bourgeois legal paraphernalia.[64]

The theory of the withering away of state and law remains an element in visions of the future communist society, but now merely as a myth. That does not mean that it lacks all significance. Some observers of Soviet law have, for example, strongly emphasized its pedagogical, educational character. The reason given for this emphasis has been that a future communist society freed from state power and legal coercion would presuppose that the citizens had internalized the basic norms of social interaction and would therefore comply with them spontaneously.[65]

In the Soviet Union a huge gap has developed between theory and practice. The development in China has been less consistent. After sharp attacks upon the judiciary and other legal personnel, all efforts to codify Chinese law came to an end. In practice, emphasis was placed on the participation of the masses in the settlement of disputes and in criminal cases. No clear line of distinction was drawn between law and morals, between private and public law or between judicial and administrative decisions. There were very few legal textbooks, and those that did exist were very limited in scope. However, some lawyers were trained, and legal development in China could have been shaped in accordance with the Marxian legal theory while at the same time being deeply rooted in old Chinese traditions and in Confucianism.[66]

Since Mao's death and the ousting of the 'Gang of Four', the development in China has taken a new turn. Legal institutions are being rebuilt, and it seems that the theory of the withering away of state and law has become obsolete in China too.

A sociological definition of the concept of law?

Theories of law that attempt to define the concept of law are of concern to sociologists for two reasons. They may, for one thing, be considered part of an ideology with empirical roots in certain social forces and interests. We have already pointed to some relationships of this kind that might contribute to an understanding of why certain theories emerge under specific social conditions. From this point of view, the sociologist is concerned with the genealogy of such theories, not with their validity or truth. However, the proposed definitions of the concept of law can also provide leads for fruitful sociological analysis by pointing to phenomena worthy of investigation – the codes, the courts and judges, general legal consciousness, etc.

A sociological analysis cannot, without reservations, be circumscribed by the definitions of traditional legal scholarship. Such definitions are determined by the search for the criteria of validity: what norms and decisions are to be considered positive law? The sociologist may be interested in many norms and decisions that cannot be considered to be part of positive law. Bills that do not pass through the legislature, the proposals for conciliation presented by judges, police methods that have no legal authority, the advice offered by legal counsel to their clients – all these phenomena belong to the 'legal system' in the sociological sense. Where the borderlines ought to be drawn is not clear, and the question is of limited interest. It seems neither necessary nor fruitful to attempt to offer a sociological definition of law.

The tasks of the law

The ambiguities and contradictions that are inherent in the concept of law are related to the fact that legal rules, as well as the enforcement of the law, serve different functions. One might, somewhat arbitrarily, distinguish five: the law is a means of governance, a way of shaping the behaviour of the citizens; it is a device for distributing resources and burdens in society; it serves to safeguard expectations; it deals with conflicts and contributes to their solution; it expresses ideals and values.

These tasks and mechanisms overlap. The expression of ideals in a statute may serve as a means of governance but may also be an expression of pure ideology, a social façade removed from the realities of the matter. Governance and distribution overlap considerably, while conflict resolution is linked with the task of steering at the same time as it has implications for the distribution of resources and burdens.

By steering we refer to a mode of influencing the behaviour of individuals through sanctions, negative or positive. Negative sanctions comprise more than penalties; they include compensation, confiscation, invalidation, certain fees and taxes to the extent that these have the aim of influencing the behaviour of people or actually have such an effect. Such means may also have other tasks, however – for instance, distribution. The award of an old-age pension is not intended to influence a pensioner's behaviour in any way. Nevertheless, if the size of the pension is related to the duration of former gainful employment, it may be viewed as a reward that motivates individuals to seek such employment and to remain in it longer than they might otherwise.

There can be little doubt that the pension system is part of a mechanism for the distribution of resources. With respect to the burdens placed on citizens, taxation is a very important means of distribution, but it may also be viewed as a vehicle for social steering, with intended or unintended consequences. One of the unintended consequences may be that progressive taxation may deter some people from doing useful work that they might have done under a different tax structure. On the other hand, some might claim that it may be appropriate to deter some people from straining themselves to achieve a very high income. In this context I simply want to point out that there are serious problems connected with any attempt to classify legal rules in accordance with a neat scheme of functions or tasks.

The German sociologist Luhmann has argued that the safeguarding of securing of social expectations is the most important task of the law.[67] Expectation is a central concept in general sociology, since it is the mechanism for transmitting the system of norms and roles in society. The significance of law in this context is betokened by the frequent references to predictability in the legal literature. The function of legal rules is to secure predictability in interaction between citizens and, not least, in their relations with public authorities. This latter type of predictability is a significant aspect of the rule of law, implying a guarantee against the arbitrary exertion of coercive state power.

It is possible to regard the safeguarding of expectations as an extension of the task of resolving conflicts, as a means of preventing conflicts and disputes. True, predictability can prevent disputes and ligitation. However, the securing of expectations is also closely linked with the task of governance. Predictability is not merely a question of communicating to people what they may expect to happen under specified conditions. The authorities will also attempt to make predictions come true through the enforcement of rules – for example, by collecting debts through the invocation of legal measures.

The safeguarding of expectations may have a particularly important function to fulfil in private law. Private law is not a means of governing behaviour. It has much in common with the rules of chess. It provides the rules of the game without making particular moves obligatory.

The resolution of conflicts is a task that in recent years has attracted a great deal of attention, especially among ethnographers with an interest in law. While governance and distribution are tasks that depend upon legislation and the existence of a state, the resolution of conflicts takes place whether or not a state framework exists. It has therefore lent itself to comparative analyses of modern societies and societies without a written language or an organized state. However, some of these comparisons may have over-emphasized the conflict-solving role of our courts. In criminal cases they may be considered a means of governance rather than of dispute settlement. Also in many civil suits (for example, those concerning the collection of debts) conflict remains in the background, and the distributive task is the primary one.

Law is bound up with ideals, but some of these may be so abstract that it is quite difficult to consider them part of a steering mechanism. Justice, equality and the rule of law are terms replete with ambiguity, hard to translate into an agreed description of reality. Such words are a symbolically important part of the ideology of a society and furnish the basis for a technique of argumentation.

If we examine law as a technique of argumentation, our frame of reference shifts from society at large to law as a weapon in the hands of combating parties. The sources of law, legislation, custom, precedents and so on become arsenals from which munition is selected in accordance with partisan interests. True, this technique is embedded in a style of reasoning that is exhibited in judicial opinions delivered with an intent to serve non-partisan societal interests.

When two contending parties present their legal arguments in an adversary process, this may or may not represent an adequate means to aid the court in its fact- and law-finding task. Toulmin has pointed to the judicial process as a model for logical argumentation,[68] thus emphasizing the non-partisan character of legal arguments. As a supplement to this, or as an alternative, I want to draw attention to the fact that arguments in a legal mould may be put at the service of interests of a partisan kind. Even if such arguments do not convince the judges, they may constitute effective ammunition in a propaganda campaign. The declarations and espousals of principles in various constitutions may serve as an arsenal for legal argumentation even if these clauses cannot be considered to be positive law. In the last chapter I shall return to this point in a discussion of human rights.

Notes

1 W. H. Auden, *Collected Poems* (London: Faber & Faber, 1976), p. 208.

2 Rodney Needham (ed.), *Right and Left: Essays on Dual Symbolic Classification* (Chicago: University of Chicago Press, 1974).

3 Fritz Metzger, 'Germ. ga-laga-n.: An log. n. P1. "geltendes Recht, Gesetz(e), Satzung, Bestimmung(en)"', *Zeitschrift für Vergleichende Sprachforschung,* 87 (1973), pp. 22–5.

4 Joseph Needham, *The Grand Titration: Science and Society in East and West* (Toronto: University of Toronto Press, 1970).

5 George M. Calhoun, *Greek Legal Science* (Oxford: Oxford University Press, 1944), pp. 78–80.

6 *Knoph's oversikt over Norges rett* (Knoph's Survey of Norwegian Law) (Oslo: Universitetsforlaget, 1975), pp. 1–2.

7 Albert K. R. Kiralfy, *The English Legal System,* 4th edn. (London: Sweet & Maxwell, 1967), pp. 2–3.

8 *Defensor Pacis* (The Defender of Peace), translated and with an introduction by Alan Gewirth (New York: Columbia University Press, 1967), p. xxxvi.

9 Niccolò Machiavelli, *The Prince* (New York: Mentor Books, 1952), p. 28. (First published 1532.)

10 Wolfgang Friedmann, *Legal Theory,* 5th edn. (London: Stevens & Sons, 1967), p. 258.

11 John Austin, *The Province of Jurisprudence Determined* (London: Weidenfeld & Nicolson, 1971), p. 133. (First published 1832.)

12 Rudolph von Ihering, *Der Zweck im Recht* (Leipzig: Breitkopf & Härtel, 1893), vol. 1, p. 322.

13 Rudolph von Ihering, *Geist des Römischen Rechts* (Leipzig: Breitkopf & Härtel, 1871), vol. 3. pp. 317ff.

14 Rudolph Sohm, *Institutionen. Ein Lehrbuch der Geschichte und des Systems des Römischen Privatrechts,* 8th and 9th edn. (Leipzig: Duncker & Humblot, 1899), p. 23.

15 H. L. A. Hart, *The Concept of Law* (Oxford: Oxford University Press, 1961), esp. pp. 97ff.

16 Ingemar Hedenius, *Om rätt och moral* (On Law and Morals) (Stockholm: Tiden Förlag, 1941), pp. 14ff.
17 ibid., p. 87.
18 ibid., p. 89.
19 ibid., p. 96.
20 Karl Olivecrona, *Rättsordningen. Idéer och fakta* (The Legal Order: Ideas and Facts) (Lund: C. W. K. Gleerūp, 1966), p. 279.
21 ibid., p. 265.
22 Alf Ross, *On Law and Justice* (London: Stevens & Sons, 1958), p. 35.
23 ibid., pp. 35–6.
24 ibid., p. 34.
25 Anders Vilhelm Lundstedt, *Föreläsningar över valda delar av obligationsrätten* (Lectures on the Law of Obligations), I and II (Uppsala: L. Norblads Bokhandel, 1920–1).
26 Per Olof Ekelöf, *Straffet, skådestandet och vitet* (Punishment, Damages and Fines) (Uppsala: Uppsala Universitets Årsskrift, 1942).
27 Karl Olivecrona, *Om lagen och staten* (On Law and the State) (Lund: C. W. K. Gleerūp, 1940), esp. p. 143.
28 In recent years Alf Ross has also discussed the functions of the penal system and has expressed general support for the theories of moral-building developed by the Uppsala school: *Skyld, ansvar og straf* (Guilt, Responsibility and Punishment) (Copenhagen: Berlingske Forlag, 1970), pp. 145, 148.
29 William Twining, *Karl Llewellyn and the Realist Movement* (London: Weidenfeld & Nicolson, 1973), p. 376.
30 *The Nature and Sources of Law* (New York: Lemcke, 1909), p. 84.
31 W. W. Cook, 'The logical and legal basis of the conflict of law', *Yale Law Journal* (1924), p. 457.
32 Karl Llewellyn, *The Bramble Bush* (New York: Oceana, 1930), p. 12. Twining has shown convincingly, however, that this cannot be taken to be *the* definition of law in Llewellyn's work: Twining, *Karl Llewellyn and the Realist Movement,* pp. 148ff.
33 Twining, *Karl Llewellyn and the Realist Movement.*
34 Karl Llewellyn and E. Adamson Hoebel, *The Cheyenne Way* (Norman, Okla.: University of Oklahoma Press, 1941); Underhill Moore and Charles C. Callahan, *Law and Learning Theory* (New Haven: Yale University Press, 1943).
35 Twining, *Karl Llewellyn and the Realist Movement,* p. 376.
36 ibid., pp. 26ff.
37 For the American situation, see Alan Hunt, *The Sociological Movement in Law* (London: Macmillan, 1978), pp. 58–9.
38 Cf. A. P. D'Entrèves, *Natural Law,* 2nd edn. (London: Hutchinson, 1979).
39 Hugo Grotius, *Laws of War and Peace* (1625).
40 Gustav Radbruch, *Rechtsphilosophie* (Stuttgart: K. F. Koehle Verlag, 1956), pp. 347ff.
41 Werner Maihofer (ed.), *Naturrecht oder Rechtspositivismus?* (Bad Homburg vor der Höhe: Hermann Gentner Verlag, 1962).
42 Gray Dorsey (ed.), *Equality and Freedom: International and Comparative Jurisprudence* (New York: Oceana/Leiden: A. W. Sijthoff, 1977).
43 Ross, *On Law and Justice,* p. 274.
44 ibid.
45 ibid., p. 284.
46 Torstein Eckhoff, *Justice: its Determinants in Social Interaction* (Rotterdam: Rotterdam University Press, 1974).
47 John Rawls, *A Theory of Justice* (Cambridge, Mass.: The Belknap Press of Harvard University Press, 1971), p. 3.

48 ibid., p. 12.
49 ibid., p. 389.
50 Cf. Friedmann, *Legal Theory*, pp. 209, 213.
51 Roscoe Pound, 'Sociology of law', in Georges Gurvitch and Wilbert E. Moore (eds.), *Twentieth Century Sociology* (New York: Philosophical Library, 1945).
52 Auguste Comte, *The Positive Philosophy* (London: Eckler, 1896), pp. 218–32. Cf. also Julius Stone, *Social Dimensions of Law and Justice* (London: Stevens & Sons, 1966), pp. 470ff.
53 Herbert Spencer, *The Man versus the State*, ed. Donald Macrae (Harmondsworth: Penguin, 1969), pp. 112ff.
54 William Graham Sumner, *Folkways* (Boston: Ginn, 1906). p. 77.
55 Leo von Petrazycki, 'Methodologie der Theorien des Rechts und der Moral', *Opera Acad. univ. iurisprud. comp.*, Ser. 2, Fasc. 2 (Paris, 1933).
56 Pitrim A. Sorokin, *Society, Culture and Personality* (New York: Cooper Square Publishers, 1962), pp. 71ff.
57 Eugen Ehrlich, *Fundamental Principles of the Sociology of Law* (New York: Russell & Russell, 1962).
58 It should be mentioned here that there is an influential trend within the social anthropological tradition that also conceives of law as norms built into the everyday interaction of people. Malinowski was a typical exponent of this type of theory: see Bronislaw Malinowski, *Crime and Custom in Savage Society* (London: Routledge & Kegan Paul, 1926).
59 Harold Ofstad, 'Om deskriptive definisjoner av begrepet "rettsregel". En sammenligning mellom Hans Kelsen's og Alf Ross' definisjoner' (On descriptive definitions of the concept of 'legal norm'. A comparison of Hans Kelsen's and Alf Ross' definitions), *Tidsskrift for rettsvidenskap*, 65 (1952), p. 79.
60 Knud Illum, *Lov og ret* (Law and Statute) (Copenhagen: Nyt nordisk forlag Arnold Būsck, 1945), p. 53.
61 Friedrich Engels, '*Der Ursprung der Familie, des Privateigentums und des Staats*', in Karl Marx/Friedrich Engels, *Werke* (Berlin: Dietz Verlag, 1962), vol. 21, esp. pp. 166–8.
62 V. I. Lenin, *The State and Revolution* (New York: International Publishers, 1932).
63 E. B. Pashukanis, 'The general theory of law and Marxism', in Hugh W. Babb and John N. Hazard (eds.), *Soviet Legal Philosophy* (Cambridge, Mass.: Harvard University Press, 1951), pp. 111–225.
64 Cf. Eugene Kamenka and Alice Erh-Soon Tay, 'Beyond the French Revolution: communist socialism and the concept of law', *University of Toronto Law Journal*, 21 (1971), pp. 109–40; Daniel Tarschys, *Beyond the State* (Stockholm: Läromedelsförlaget, 1972).
65 Cf. James L. Hildebrand, 'The sociology of Soviet law: the heuristic and "parental functions"', *Case Western Reserve Law Review*, 22 (1971), pp. 157–229.
66 Jerome Alan Cohen (ed.), *Contemporary Chinese Law: Research Problems and Perspectives* (Cambridge, Mass.: Harvard University Press, 1970); Alice Erh-Soon Tay, 'Law in communist China', parts 1–3, *Sydney Law Review*, 6, 7, 8 (1971, 1972).
67 Niklas Luhmann, *Rechtssoziologie* (Reinbek bei Hamburg: Rowohlt, 1972), pp. 31ff.
68 Stephen Toulmin, *The Uses of Argument* (Cambridge: Cambridge University Press, 1974), pp. 7–8, 15–17, 41–3, 96, 141–2.

CHAPTER 2

The rule of law

The rule of law (*Rechtsstaat, Rechtssicherheit, rettssikkerhet*) refers to law in a sense that is more restricted than when the concern is the concept or nature of law in general. However, even in this context the term 'law' covers a rather disparate set of concepts. Among these there are a few that occur more often than others.

According to A. V. Dicey's influential definition, the rule of law requires that 'no man is punishable or can be lawfully made to suffer in body or goods except for a distinct breach of law established in the ordinary legal manner before the ordinary courts of the land.'[1] And further: 'every man, whatever be his rank or condition is subject to the ordinary law of the realm and amenable to the jurisdiction of the ordinary tribunals.'[2]

Dicey was adamant that the administrative powers, the executive, should govern under the supervision of the ordinary courts. In his view, a system of administrative courts, as in France, represented a breach of the rule of law. For this standpoint he does not seem to have the support of modern scholars in the field of administrative law;[3] however, his general definition may approach the stable nucleus of a variety of definitions of the rule of law.

In his recent text on administrative law Wade begins by recognizing the variety of meanings associated with the rule of law: 'The rule of law has a number of different meanings and corollaries. Its primary meaning is that everything must be done according to law.'[4] Specifically, he implies that acts of a government authority that infringe an individual's liberty must be authorized by an Act of Parliament. He adds, however, that this is the principle of legality and that the rule of law demands more, namely, 'that government should be conducted within a framework of recognized rules and principles which restrict discretionary powers'.[5]

A crucial point is how, and how much, this discretionary power should be restricted. This brings Wade too to attribute to the courts a central function in upholding the rule of law:

> disputes as to the legality of acts are to be decided by judges who are wholly independent of the executive . . . The right to carry a dispute with the government before the ordinary courts, manned by judges of the highest independence, is an important element in the Anglo-American concept of the rule of law.[6]

From a strictly logical point of view, these definitions of the rule of law, which I take to be fairly representative of the common law tradition, are unsatisfactory and incomplete. They define the rule of law in a somewhat circular fashion by referring to other concepts that depend upon a previous conception of legality. Dicey refers to the establishment of law 'in the ordinary legal manner', and the two authors' reference to the courts contains no specified requirements with respect to their mode of operation. The definitions refer, however, to a well-known, traditional conception of the courts within the English legal system. Some implications of this will be elaborated in the following chapters.

The Anglo-American term 'rule of law' seems to correspond quite closely to the German terms *Rechtssicherheit* and *Rechtsstaat* as well as the Scandinavian terms *rettssikkerhet* and *rettsstat.* A leading nineteenth-century German proponent of the idea of the *Rechtsstaat,* Georg Jellinek, expresses this conception of the rule of law thus:

> Every legal rule also constitutes a guarantee to the legal subjects that the state is itself under an obligation for as long as the rule remains in force. . . . Before its subjects the state commits itself through the creative legal act – irrespective of how the law originates – to apply and enforce the law.[7]

In this conception there is a self-limitation on the state and a restriction upon the arbitrary and discretionary exertion of public authority. It may not, however, be purely accidental that Jellinek, working within the framework of a strongly codified legal system, does not specifically emphasize the role of the courts in a *Rechtsstaat.*

A more recent exposition of the idea of the *Rechtsstaat* is closer to Anglo-American conceptions of the rule of law and refers specifically to the courts. In Coing's opinion, the *Rechtsstaat* represents an attempt to harmonize the demands for individual justice with the necessary enforcement of state authority. The relationship of power between those who govern and their subjects is regulated by the idea of law. More specifically, this entails the need to ensure that the power of the state is not concentrated in one set of hands. A division of powers must prevail. All state power must be based upon law and restricted by law to the pursuit of a specified purpose. All acts of the state must be open to control by the citizens, who must have recourse to a legal suit against the state before independent courts and through elected representatives.[8]

In the German *Encyclopaedia of the Social Sciences* the double meaning of the term *Rechtsstaat* is emphasized. One sense is characterized as formal and refers to the legal ordering and limitation on the uses of governmental power and the controlling power of independent and authoritative courts. The second meaning relates to a wide concept of social justice. The term *Rechtssicherheit* (legal certainty and protection) is related to the former, and formal, meaning of *Rechtsstaat.*[9]

Although the equivalent general concept of *rettssikkerhet* (legal certainty) plays a prominent part in Scandinavian public debate in various contexts, it has not been thoroughly or systematically treated by legal theorists or constitutional lawyers. However, the three leading Norwegian legal authorities in this field, Andenaes, Castberg and Eckhoff, have presented their views of the concept.

During the German occupation of Norway Andenaes formulated a dual approach to the problem:

> With respect to *rettssikkerhet,* one may have two things in mind. First, one may think of protection against interference with one's legal rights by other citizens. Secondly, there is the question of protection against the abusive and arbitrary exertion of power by the state itself.[10]

Andenaes's dual approach may be related to the terminological difference between 'rule of law' and *rettssikkerhet.* The term *sikkerhet* has connotations of certainty as well as protection and comfort. For a criminal lawyer it may be natural to consider too the protection of life and property against illegal assaults. The two types of *rettssikkerhet* may lead to conflicting policies, however. A strong emphasis upon protection for potential victims of crime, a cry for 'law and order', may easily lead to the neglect of legal guarantees for suspects and defendants.

However, in the Norwegian theoretical literature the emphasis is on protection against arbitrariness in the execution of state power. In Castberg's view, the principal idea behind the notion of the *rettsstat* is that the constitution and the legal system as a whole should protect everybody against arbitrariness. Decisions ought to be made not on the basis of personal opinions or whims but according to the principle of formal equality. Arbitrariness is unjust, and injustice should be prevented.[11]

In pursuing Castberg's injunction against arbitrary acts of government Eckhoff is more specific. He emphasizes not only the predictability of legal status and the defensibility of legal interests but also equality and justice. He states, with specific reference to administrative law: 'The first condition for *rettssikkerhet* is that the administrative agencies are *bound by rules* when they make decisions affecting (physical or juridical) persons.'[12] The second necessary condition has to do with procedural requirements: 'These requirements imply that the decisions be left to unbiased persons, that private parties must be given ample opportunity to defend their interests, and that there must be access to review by a superior authority, preferably the courts.'[13]

Andenaes emphasizes the significance of judicial review in even stronger and more general terms: 'By us it is generally recognized that an independent judiciary is one of the most important guarantees of *rettssikkerhet* in society.'[14]

Political scientists too have stressed the formal, procedural aspect of the rule of law: 'The rule of law in its English context has (like due process of law and natural justice) been mainly expounded . . . as a procedural concept.'[15] Carl Friedrich, for example, concurs with this emphasis upon procedure, arguing against Dicey that 'in Continental Europe it is through such administrative courts alone that the rule of law, the *rechtsstaat,* or government according to law, can be made secure.'[16] Friedrich attributes, quite generally, great political significance to the courts' specific mode of treating problems:

In summing up what has been shown in regard to the settling of disputes, we may say that such dispute-settling is perhaps the most basic kind of political process, without which political order is inconceivable . . . It was shown that the basic design of this process consists of an accuser, a defender and a settler, and that the settler needs power, authority and legitimacy in order to be effective.[17]

The rule of law has attracted more interest from philosophers of law and jurisprudential scholars than from legal sociologists. There are also sociologists of law who have dealt with the problem, however. Selznick, for example, treats the term 'legality' as though it were synonymous with the rule of law.[18] He emphasizes restraint of official power as the essential element in the rule of law and goes on to underline the predominance of procedural principles: 'Legality has to do mainly with how policies and rules are made and applied rather than with their content.'[19] He is aware that legality is a limited ideal: 'Legality is a part of justice, but only a part.'[20] Justice is concerned with the content of rules, and too much commitment to procedural integrity may undo substantive justice.[21] Nevertheless, there are times when the ideal of legality determines the content of a legal rule or doctrine. This occurs when the purpose of the rule is precisely to implement that ideal, the most obvious illustration being the elaboration of procedural rules of pleading and evidence.[22]

Although the proper aim of the legal order is to minimize the arbitrary element in decision-making,[23] Selznick holds that '"discretion" is compatible with the rule of law when it remains essentially judicial rather than administrative.'[24] Again we encounter a strong reliance upon court proceedings, and Selznick provides a clue to what is so special about the courts: 'The primary function of adjudication is to discover the legal co-ordinates of a particular situation. That is a far cry from manipulating the situation to achieve a desired outcome.'[25] I think he has in mind the difference between the subsuming of a factual state under a rule and the choice of means to achieve a goal, based upon assumptions about causal relationship. We shall follow up this line of reasoning in chapters 3 and 4.

Mangabeira Unger distinguishes between three concepts of law: customary law, regulatory or bureaucratic law and, finally, the legal order. The legal order is a narrower concept than the other two, and it is closely related to the rule of law.[26] The autonomy of this kind of law, is crucial, and it is secured by the existence of specialized institutions whose main task is adjudication (for example, the courts). Interestingly, Mangabeira Unger concurs with Selznick in his emphasis upon the special methodology of adjudication. The courts justify their acts in a way that differs from methods used in other disciplines and practices: 'This means that legal reasoning has a method or style to differentiate it from scientific explanation and from moral, political and economic discourse.'[27] He goes on to explain how the rule of law, a relatively rare phenomenon in human societies, came into being in the modern Western liberal state.[28]

The contributions of these different scholars strengthen the conviction that the situation and function of the courts, procedural and methodological issues, are focal in any discussion of the rule of law. It cannot be denied, however, that less tangible and wider issues have been associated with the concept. The general protection of vital human interests against unlawful attack has been mentioned. The demand for equality before the law, maybe even equality generally, appears quite often in the literature on the rule of law. Democratic representation has also been mentioned, an ideal which, when applied to the judiciary, sometimes clashes with the demand for autonomy.

One of the widest conceptions of the rule of law in the German version of the *Rechtsstaat* was presented by Fichte nearly two centuries ago. This *Rechtsstaat* is a far cry from the 'night-watchman's state' that became the typical embodiment of the rule of law. Fichte's state is obliged to ensure: '(a) that the necessities of life are produced in a quantity proportionate to the number of citizens; (b) that every one can satisfy his needs through work'.[29]

An echo of this notion can be heard in the resolutions adopted during various meetings of the International Commission of Jurists. In these resolutions the rule of law is given such wide scope that it covers nearly everything associated with social justice. The following quotation illustrates the point:

> 8. The International Commission of Jurists has, since its foundation, been dedicated to the support and advancement throughout the world of those principles of justice which constitute the basis of the Rule of Law. The term 'Rule of Law', as defined and interpreted by the various Congresses sponsored by the International Commission of Jurists, seeks to emphasize that mere legality is not enough and that the broader conceptions of justice as distinct from positive legal rules are embraced by the term and, indeed, provide its more vital aspect.[30]

This was followed up by a reference to the Declaration of Delhi (1959), which contains this statement:

the Rule of Law is a dynamic concept for the expansion and fulfilment of which jurists are primarily responsible and which should be employed not only to safeguard and advance the civil and political rights of the individual in a free society, but also to establish social, economic, educational and cultural conditions under which his legitimate aspirations and dignity may be realized.[31]

This heavy emphasis upon a broad conception of social justice must of course, be understood in the international context of these meetings. The Third World was well represented, and its problems were discussed; such discussion must highlight the relative irrelevancy of the formal application of the rule of law in countries beset by massive poverty, disease and premature death.

Even in this context, however, it turns out to be difficult for an assembly of lawyers to stray from a narrow professional path, as is evident from a statement on the relationship between the rule of law and traditional Chinese and Korean legal theories. Since communist Chinese legal theory in these respects corresponds with the Confucian concept of law, the following pronouncement must be viewed as a rejection of the communist experience, notwithstanding the great strides that the Chinese have made with respect to social welfare, health, economic modernization and educational achievements:

[Confucian philosophy] was very much a philosophy of the rule of men and not of law; its ideals were rendered incarnate in an intellectual elite of benevolent philosophers. The states which attempted to realize these Confucian principles were characterized by:

(a) Relatively few statutes or similar materials; such as there were, were couched in broad general language, which tended to be an injunction to comply with certain ethical principles rather than detailed substantive legislation. Normally, these statutes remained in effect for long periods of time without extensive amendment.

(b) Non-publication of administrative materials circulated internally within the government between officials.

(c) A bureaucracy, assumed to be drawn from the intellectual elite, which occupied one of the highest, if not the highest, prestige position within the society.

(d) Unification of the judicial and the legislative functions in the hands of the executive.

(e) A general dislike for litigation felt by the people and a corresponding lack of 'rights-consciousness' fostered by active policies of the government. Use of unofficial means of resolving disputes, such as mediation, was encouraged in place of recourse to courts.

(f) Non-existence of a legal profession. Those who sought to argue principles of law while representing the interests of parties were looked upon as pettifoggers and parasites and as making no useful contribution to society.

81. Attitudes similar to the Korean and Chinese attitudes have contributed in varying degrees to the total or partial breakdown of the Rule of Law in other parts of Asia.[32]

According to the classical, 'pure' Marxist theory of law and state, there should be no room in a communist society for the rule of law in the narrow sense, only for social justice. Since law is a bourgeois contraption, aimed at the suppression of the toiling masses, a complete abandonment of law and the withering away of the state was the Utopian ideal. However, the actual development of the Soviet state, and other Marxist states as well, has led to a modification (to put it mildly) of this theory. A concept of 'socialist legality' has emerged, and it must be seen as the communist answer to the challenge of the Western rule of law.[33]

In the initial revolutionary stages of emerging Soviet society an anarchist theory of the state and law corresponded to a situation characterized by the relative absence of law and order and frequent changes in government policy. In strict logic this was not so. Lenin's theory of the withering away of the state referred to a future communist stage, while the socialist stage, the dictatorship of the proletariat, allowed for the continued use of law as a means of suppression directed against the class enemy.

With the development of the Soviet economy and social structure generally, the demand for legal rules and a machinery of enforcement must have been irresistible. The recognized brutality and arbitrariness of the Stalin regime fuelled the demand that state power should be exercised according to the demands of 'socialist legality'.

Even leaving practice aside, one cannot without qualification equate socialist legality with the rule of law. According to Selznick:

The rule of law is a practical ideal, which is to say it rests in part on pessimistic premises regarding the nature of man and society. 'Free

> government', wrote Thomas Jefferson, 'is founded in jealousy, and not in confidence, it is jealousy, and not confidence, which prescribes limited constitutions, to bind down those whom we are obliged to trust with power . . . in questions of power, then, let no more be heard of confidence in man, but bind him down from mischief by the chains of the Constitution.' The assumption is that no man, no group of men, is to be trusted with unlimited power. No amount of wisdom or good will can justify a transfer of untrammelled power to mortal men.[34]

This view of man as essentially self-seeking and competitive and of society as necessarily torn by conflicts between subjects and ruling elites is not accepted in Marx's theory. Whether this description of man and society fits depends upon the class structure and, ultimately, on the mode of production. In an advanced socialist society the prevailing state is one of harmony of interests between those who govern and those who are governed: the absence of any doctrine of 'division of powers' and other striking deviations from the practical implications of the Western conception of legality.

We have seen that the independence of the judiciary is crucial to rule of law ideology. Quite apart from recruitment procedures, party ties, informal pressures, etc., there is a clear and formal breach with this principle in the Soviet legal system, as demonstrated by the powers of the Prokuratura. One aspect of the Prokuratura's function is similar to that of the office of the Attorney General, the head of the prosecutorial arm of the government. It functions also, however, in an Ombudsman capacity. The Prokuratura is authorized to review administrative decisions. In this respect it represents an approximation to the Western, and especially the American, theory of checks and balances or countervailing forces, a theory of governmental constraint.[35]

However, the courts have no authority to review the constitutionality of legislative enactments. And, what may be more significant, the Prokuratura may subject even plenary decisions of the Supreme Court to review by the Presidium of the Supreme Soviet. This is certainly an important limitation upon the independence of the courts. It may, however, be objected that the difference between the Soviet and the Western conception is a mere formality. Certainly, it is a formality, but no *mere* formality, in that the difference does have practical consequences.

I do not exclude the possibility that some governments that are dedicated, in principle, to the rule of law are in a position unduly to secure judicial conformity to their interests and policies. This depends, as Marxists would quite correctly claim with reference to Engels, upon the state of the class struggle. In societies where governing elites feel threatened by a frustrated and disgruntled majority, the judges may, out of identification with their social class, be swayed towards obedience to the executive in times of crisis. Furthermore, it may be claimed that even in liberal, social democratic states the independence of the courts is of very limited significance for most defendants in criminal cases and in most routine civil law cases. Nevertheless, the exceptional case is important.

The rule of law as an answer to human needs

In the preceding pages I have tried to highlight certain aspects of an ideological fragment called the 'rule of law'. What it corresponds to in social reality is a different matter. At this stage, however, it may be appropriate to look briefly at the genesis of this ideology. It has its roots in the same general human needs and dispositions that have secured an appreciation of law as a byword for preferred and highly valued social arrangements. More specifically, the rule of law and, even more clearly, *Rechtssicherheit* seems to answer to the need for certainty, predictability, order and safety. It is a normative institution closely attuned to the mini-max principle.[36]

Jerome Frank developed this point of view into a fairly elaborate theory about the belief in legal certainty as a father surrogate. According to Frank, there is ample reason to be sceptical about the ability of the courts to discover the truth – what has really happened – in the cases they deal with. A failure to establish the facts of the case correctly implies uncertainty and lack of predictability in the implementation of the law, even if the rules themselves are clear and unambiguous. Frank wonders, then, why people still have faith in the rule of law and the authority of the courts. He ascribes this unfounded confidence to a strong need for certainty in the shape of an infallible father figure.[37]

It seems reasonable to assume that people in general have a craving for points of certainty in life, which is, and probably always has been, beset by risks and imponderables. To meet this craving through the operation of social institutions is difficult, even if it is in the interests of those who decide such matters to make the attempt. However, at the symbolic level beliefs and fragments of ideologies have developed that promise a level of security and predictability that renders the hazards of social life more tolerable than they would otherwise be.

It is in this general context that we must place the nebulous doctrine of the rule of law. It is, however, clear that this vague but powerful demand for certainty and comfort in a world of risk and unforeseeable change could be met by many different conceptions and images of law. The fact that the answer is couched in this particular terminology and focuses so much upon courts and procedure needs a different explanation.

There seems to be a fair amount of agreement that legality in this particular sense is a concomitant of the emergence of the modern liberal state and the market economy. In the market ideology of Adam Smith and the theory of the division of powers of Montesquieu or Jefferson there is a parallel emphasis upon competition. Both rest upon similar premises concerning the self-seeking nature of man, which can, however, be turned to the common good by the proper legal arrangements. What the legal protection of property and contracts can do to the economy, the representative system and the division of state powers can do to the polity.

This is not the place to attempt a systematic sociological explanation of the evolution of rule of law ideology. It should be noted, however, that a detailed elaboration of the doctrine and its implications has been a dominant concern of the legal profession. The emergence of the rule of law doctrine took place at the same time as the expansion and consolidation of the legal profession intensified and as systematic education was introduced in several European countries. The rule of law has been appropriated by the legal experts as their spiritual property. However diffuse, emotional and simple the lay demand for the rule of law, lawyers have convinced themselves and many others that it takes an expert trained in law to form an intelligent opinion about what it means in concrete practical situations.

Internal contradictions in the rule of law

Conflicts between the rule of law and efficiency have often been pointed out. If a broad concept of the rule of law is adopted, it will include, for example, the effective policing of areas threatened by crime. Then tension will arise between two considerations, both pertaining to the rule of law. I shall say no more of this in the present context. However, tensions may also arise in connection with the narrower concept, that which refers to the guarantees against governmental arbitrariness and the need for courts.

It is realistic to assume that conflicts of interest between citizens and the state may occur – for example, when a law is being enforced. The rule of law requires in such instances that the citizen is entitled to demand a certain thoroughness in the procedure that is applied to his case. Concretely, this may imply access to documents, the right of appeal to higher authority or to a tribunal, etc. An eventual legal suit against the state may follow from the definition of the state as a separate subject, according to private law, in its capacity as buyer, seller, landlord, tenant, creditor, debtor, etc., or from the general authority of the courts to review aspects of administrative action.

Such principles provide the citizen with legal weapons with which to fight the government's own decisions. The initiative is left to the aggrieved private individual, however, which means that there may be great inequalities in the utilization of such weapons. Formal equality of opportunity to sue the government is unequally exploited. Also, the rule of law depends to a greater or lesser extent upon market relations, which regulate access to legal counsel. The establishment of free legal aid in various forms represents attempts to remedy this course of inequality. Such reforms are aimed explicitly at fostering the rule of law.

To the extent that equality before the law and predictability also refer to real access to procedural remedies, such inequalities represent infringements of the rule of law. The more complex and thorough the manner in which the legal process is construed in the name of the rule of law, the more pronounced this inequality may become. Delay in court can also introduce an arbitrary element in the consequences of litigation, although this does not necessarily lead to systematic inequalities, but rather to the random distribution of favours and burdens. On the whole, the time dimension is poorly controlled and scarcely considered as an aspect of the rule of law, although a speedy decision may be a vital aspect of access to judicial review (possibly an instance of the best being the enemy of the good). Elaborate procedures may consume so much time that they will be of use only to the few who can afford to wait and see.

Nulla poena sine lege

The prototypical derivation from the rule of law is the principle of 'no punishment without a law', which enshrines a demand for that predictability which depends on a warning that specified types of transgression will be countered by penalties. The principle also implies a demand for equality. A law is a general rule that establishes equality among those who fulfil, or fail to fulfil, conditions established by the rule. There is a third implication of this principle: the assumption of centralization and co-ordination. A law is not just any general rule; it is a rule issued by the legislative body of the state.

These principles offer no guarantee of social justice – either in the sense that all citizens are given equal access to the resources of society, or in accordance with any other definable principle of justice, such as 'to each according to his ability'. It is not a necessary criterion of a *Rechtsstaat* that legislation should correspond to the legal consciousness of the population. Nor does the correspondence between general legal consciousness and the law ensure the rule of law. Under the rule of law small, deviant minorities enjoy procedural protection, however much the majority may scorn such treatment as excessive tolerance.

In order to understand better the meaning of *nulla poena sine lege* (a principle that was unknown to the Romans, incidentally), we must inquire into the meaning of the terms 'law' and 'penalty'. Let us note straightaway that the principle of legality has a somewhat broader meaning, since it includes all interference with the legal status of the citizens. It refers not merely to punishment but also to the draft, the duty to attend school, taxation and so on, which all require the authorization of the law. However, the principle of legality in this formal sense is not instituted in all states that are considered to be *Rechtsstaate* (for example, Sweden).

A central problem is what we are to understand by a law within the conception of the rule of law. It is neither a necessary nor a sufficient condition that the norm is a law in the formal constitutional sense (a Bill enacted by Parliament according to a prescribed procedure, for instance). Orders and decrees that are issued under powers delegated by a formal law do not offend the rule of law, although doubts may arise if the delegated rule-making powers are very far-reaching. On the other hand, the fact that a norm is embodied in a formally unassailable enactment by the legislature gives no absolute guarantee that the rule of law will be abided by.

I am not referring primarily to the possible unconstitutionality of a Bill – for example, that it may authorize expropriation without full compensation. The decisive criterion is that the enforcement of the law can be reviewed by the courts or according to another judicial procedure. The deviant citizen cannot, on the basis of the rule of law, demand legal protection for his deviant lifestyle. Such protection must be based on a wider conception of justice. The homosexual, for example, cannot claim, by reference to the rule of law, a right to practise homosexuality in contravention of the law and demand immunity against penal sanctions. However, the rule of law entitles him to have any official interference with his life on this count tried by a court of law, according to a certain procedure.

The principle of *nulla poena sine lege* must, as Friedrich maintains, be translated into *nullum crimen sine judice* (no crime without judgment).[38] The Norwegian Constitution, like many others, is very sparing and brief in its characterization of the courts. Strictly speaking, it offers no explicit procedural guarantees against interference from public authorities such as the police. The detailed procedural rules for criminal trials and civil litigation are found in a number of measures dealing with court administration.

The key to an understanding of the rule of law in this context is the phrase 'to judge *according* to the law'. What is a proper verdict, and what must be asked of a law in order that one may judge *according* to it? In the next two chapters we shall try to answer these questions. Chapter 3 will address primarily the organizational structure of adjudication, while chapter 4 is concerned with the kind of reasoning that is applicable to this mode of dealing with, and possibly resolving, disputes.

Traditional corollaries of the rule of law

The rule of law doctrine may be viewed as one dominant element in an interconnected cluster of ideological fragments. We shall look at the most salient of these.

The notion of the free market

The liberal *Rechtsstaat* was consolidated as a concomitant of the Industrial Revolution and the growth of a market economy. This development found its expression in, and was also furthered by, the emergence of a theory fathered by Adam Smith. The theory proposed that if men's actions in the market were motivated by enlightened self-interest, an invisible hand would steer the aggregate of selfish actions so as to further the common good and the wealth of nations. The interplay of demand and supply, as well as competition between the sellers, would be more beneficial than the old protectionist and mercantilist system of privileges and governmental attempts to steer the economy.[39]

The model of competition as a system of social interaction goes back a long way in history and is to be found in a wide variety of cultures in games and various forms of contest. One may distinguish between games of skill and games of chance. Both types of game are required to be in some sense just. The contest must be fair. Therefore games are set within an often elaborate framework of rules, norms stipulating what is permissible and what is forbidden. (Games were often supposed to take place within a fenced-off arena.)[40]

It is no accident that Ross, in his attempt to penetrate the core of legal phenomena, uses the game of chess as a model of the legal system. He makes a distinction between two sets of norms: the constituent and the strategic. The constituent rules are the commonly accepted rules stipulating which moves are permissible and which forbidden to those who want to participate in a game of chess. The strategic norms provide guidelines about how a player ought to proceed in order to win the game.[41] These latter rules are not authoritatively settled, however, and there may not be consensus about their content. The guardians of the game of chess have no responsibility to enforce them and need not assign priorities to them. The outcome of the game is what counts.

This metaphor provides an excellent picture of how legal rules were intended to function in the liberal law state. It was the government's task to create and enforce a set of constituent rules, to defend law and order, while simultaneously granting the citizenry the freedom to choose its own strategies within this framework. For the legal authorities the main task was to guarantee that property and contracts were respected, which meant, of course, that not all citizens were, in practice, equally protected. The ideology of the free market tended, however, to ignore the glaring inequalities found in nineteenth-century European societies.

The constituent legal rules of the market, prescribing the conditions for the valid acquisition or transfer of property, as well as for the validity of contracts, provided a basis for competition among citizens in their efforts to win the highest prizes. The means to achieve success in business could be many – ranging from great inventions, rational principles of industrial organization and hard work, to pathological stinginess, barely legal cunning and the exertion of power. However, the law itself remained silent about these strategies. The largest rewards were, by and large, distributed throughout the market. And if the state itself awarded prizes, the premises were rarely established in the shape of legal rules. Public office and the level of remuneration in the 'nightwatchman's state' were in some measure determined by market forces, partly by descent and partly by the grace of the king. The frequent use of the term 'grace' demonstrates the deviation from the demands of the rule of law on the reward side of the state's system of sanctions.

Law as a morality of duty

The market ideology and the constituent function of the law are related to another ideological element, the notion that law sets minimum standards and leaves it to other normative systems to outline the highest ideals. In the quotation from Knoph above (p. 8) this conception of law as minimum ethics is closely connected with the threat of force as a necessary quality of legal rules.

The American philosopher of law Lon Fuller has elaborated more explicitly upon the distinction between what he calls a 'morality of duty' and a 'morality of aspiration (or excellence)'.[42] By a 'morality of duty' he refers to a set of norms establishing minimum standards of behaviour. The criminal law typifies this, but it applies, in Fuller's view, to legal rules quite generally. A 'morality of aspiration (excellence)', on the other hand, embodies norms that encourage people to reach for high – perhaps unattainable – ideals. The command to love one's neighbour as oneself, mentioned by Knoph, is an example of this kind of morality.

Fuller's view is consistent with a tradition within legal theory. Nearly a century ago Georg Jellinek claimed: 'Law is nothing but the ethical minimum.'[43] He expanded this point thus:

> the law does not aim at the realization of an ethical ideal inherent in the positive content of the institution in question. The law is simply a guardian at its outer limits, so that the principle is upheld and not contradicted. Morals give the idea the fullest reality and its positive aspect; the law, on the other hand, acts on it only negatively and at its outermost periphery.[44]

A similar line of reasoning can be found in the writings of the founding father of modern Scandinavian legal scholarship, the Dane Ørsted. In a discussion of the relationship between rewards and penalties as means of directing social action, he describes compliance with the law as a 'negative virtue'.[45]

There seems to be a profound relationship between emphasis on the minimalist aspect of legal norms and the rule of law. Some of the reasons for this are easy to discern. It presents fewer problems to determine a nether limit and to register violations of that than to prescribe generally what a peak achievement should be. The opportunity for drawing a limit seems to be a prerequisite for the practical realization of the rule of law, since borderline problems feature heavily in the work of legal personnel.

Minimum standards lie within a range of behaviour with which many people are familiar, and therefore there exists a base in experience for drawing borderlines and for formulating them with a relatively high degree of precision. At the positive end of the behavioural scale there are no limits as familiar as those to be found at the bottom. This may be one reason why there is more agreement over minimum than over maximum standards. Another reason is the assumption that every adult in his right mind is capable of complying with the minimum demands of the law, while only the few and select will excel. Modern societies are characterized by a marked pluralism in the evaluation of peak performances (probably a necessary concomitant of the division of labour).

Minimum standards as found in criminal law, in the law of torts and of contract, deal primarily with interpersonal relationships. In a small circle certain individuals may be acclaimed for their performance as a good mother or father, a loving spouse or a helpful neighbour. However, the public system of approval and praise is oriented towards actions that lead to results only through complex mediating mechanisms. On these results there may be divergent opinions, depending upon the interests and values of those who observe and evaluate. People may also differ with respect to the assignment of responsibility or merit for such achievements, another reason why it is more difficult to establish laws based upon a morality of aspiration.

The rejection of rewards and the economy of sanctions

In chapter one we pointed to the vital function assigned to the use of force in definitions of law. For the most part, the authors who have voiced this view have not found it necessary to discuss explicitly why positive sanctions, rewards, are ignored as an alternative means of motivating and governing citizens. Some, however, have considered this juxtaposition of positive and negative sanctions.

In *The Prince* Machiavelli discusses the relationship between penalties and rewards as means of ruling and of maintaining power. Here we encounter a theme that we may term the 'economy of sanctions', which seems to have had a decisive influence upon theories of deterrence as a rationale for criminal prosecution. Machiavelli raises this question on behalf of the prince:

> whether it is better to be loved more than feared, or feared more than loved? The reply is, that one ought to be both feared and loved, but as it is difficult for the two to go together, it is much safer to be feared than loved, if one of the two has to be wanting.[46]

He looks upon love in this political context as a fragile flower in need of constant nourishment — through hand-outs to the populace. If these fail, the claim of obligation to the prince may be easily broken, while 'fear is maintained by a dread of punishment which never fails.' The economies of sanctioning are even more clearly indicated in the following passage:

> A prince, therefore, must not mind incurring the charge of cruelty for the purpose of keeping his subjects united and faithful; for, with a very few examples, he will be more merciful than those who, from excess of

tenderness, allow disorders to arise, from whence spring bloodshed and raping, for those as a rule injure the whole community, while the executions carried out by the prince injure only individuals.[47]

Deterrence, the use of 'a very few examples', is presented as a cheap and efficient way of maintaining order in society. This is certainly one of the basic and seminal notions in man's conception of social order and its prerequisites. It still holds sway over legislators (and electorates as well) in spite of the impressive series of government failures to achieve conformity to laws through the promulgation of threats of punishment. In part, this reliance upon deterrence has its roots in certain fundamental and universal asymmetries between rewards or resources and negative sanctions. But, it should be noted, Machiavellian and related theories of government and power are also deeply rooted in the nature of states at the dawn of the modern era, the strength of which depended to a large extent upon the size and effectiveness of a king's army.

A more surprising rejection of rewards as a means of governing is to be found in Jeremy Bentham's writings. His utilitarian theory consists in a broad, systematic and quite symmetrical presentation of pleasures and pains, their subdivisions and functions. In one place he states explicitly:

The business of government is to promote the happiness of the society, by punishing and rewarding.[48]

However, later he pronounces quite dogmatically:

If legislation interferes in a direct manner, it must be by punishment.

And he adds to this a footnote:

I say nothing in this place of reward, because it is only in a few extraordinary cases that it can be applied, and because even where it is applied, it may be doubted perhaps whether the application of it can, properly speaking, be termed an act of legislation.[49]

It is important to bear in mind the historical context when we attempt to understand why the theories of law that developed during the various phases of absolute monarchy emphasized coercion and penalties to such a degree. Their influence can be seen in theories of natural law as elsewhere. Adherents of natural law such as Grotius, Hobbes, Locke and, later on, Blackstone all emphasized the crucial role of the threat of punishment as the main vehicle for maintaining social order and curbing the antisocial tendencies of man. Blackstone believed threats to be more effective than promises of reward, and at the same time he stressed that the state lacked the resources to reward all law-abiding behaviour.[50] The same point was emphasized a few decades later when the Danish lawyer Nørregaard pointed to the fact that the law relies primarily upon penalties to secure conformity to its norms. Nørregaard claimed that 'it would be impossible for the state to reward all compliance with the law and thus procure, for example, 1000 obedient subjects instead of punishing one transgressor.'[51]

In more recent times, and in a surprisingly similar vein, the same problem has been discussed by Schwartz and Orleans:

> Sanctions are officially imposed punishments aimed at enforcement of legal obligations. They are said to constitute the core, if not the defining characteristic, of the legal order.[52]

They continue:

> Our legal system contains very few instances in which people are explicitly rewarded for compliance, rather than punished for deviance . . . for reasons of economy explicit rewards tend to be employed where only small segments of the population are supposed to be their recipients. . . . Extension of rewards to all who observe the law would be expensive, difficult to administer, and ineffective if the recipients were numerous.[53]

In apparent contrast to this, the American legal scholars Hurst and Reich have drawn attention to the 'rewarding', positive aspect of modern law. Reich especially points to the enormous growth of the modern state's command of resources and to its role as a dispenser and distributor of these resources.[54] The transition from the 'nightwatchman's state' to the industrial or post-industrial welfare or interventionist state is certainly one of the momentous events of recent history. Whether the development of the welfare state, with its vast apparatus of social, medical and educational services, contradicts or disproves Schwartz's and Orleans's denial that rewards may be an important type of legal sanction depends to some extent at least upon how we define and employ the concept of sanction.

One of the great changes that have taken place in the nature of the world in recent times, and one of the preconditions for the changing role of the state, has been the massive expansion of man's influence on his material environment, which has had significant repercussions with respect to methods of social (including legal) control. In societies with less developed material resources than those of modern industrial society, social control was exerted to a great extent through perceived magical and religious sanctions, through physical violence and, finally, through social disapproval, which impinged upon honour and the sense of personal worth. Manipulation of the material environment played a rather limited role in the arsenal of legal means of influence.

Today, however, a major vehicle of influence is provided by the numerous and varied opportunities that authorities have to extend or withhold goods, services and other resources. Most citizens, apart from a minority of down-and-outs, are enmeshed in a network of access to 'alienable goods'[55] (resources that can be taken away from them). Legal rules may stipulate the conditions under which this may be done, either as a sanction or for some other purpose such as the redistribution of income or wealth. The state is in charge of the distribution of a large share of these resources and can, to some extent, use its command of resources to reward desirable behaviour and to penalize non-compliance.

The rule of law and social inequalities

The links between the rule of law and the cluster of concomitant ideological elements, as well as the social conditions under which the *Rechtsstaat* principle gained a foothold, suggest that there may today be a gap between the ideal and the reality. While the doctrine may receive as much vocal support as it ever did, or more, the preconditions for its realization have changed a great deal. The notions of the free market and the invisible hand have been, to a greater or lesser extent, modified in Western welfare states. The legislator is no longer satisfied with establishing minimum standards of conduct but offers instead visions of a new and better society under the law, or at least under the preambles of laws. The need for sanction economy is reduced through the vastly increased wealth of the modern state. Governance through the distribution or withholding of money takes the place of governance through the threat of punishment, damages, or invalidity of attempted contractual arrangements.

The rule of law was the ideology of a rising bourgeoisie as a defence against the injustices of the feudal lords and the unpredictable despotism of absolute monarchs. Equality before the law meant the equality of those with full citizen's rights.[56] This also benefited underprivileged groups, although not to the same extent as those who were privileged in terms of property rights and their share in the spoils of the state.

In my reference above to the ambivalence of the International Commission of Jurists there are suggestions that the rule of law, in the narrow, juridical sense, favours the haves rather than the have-nots. This applies to the international scene, as is apparent from a comparison of Western states with those of the Third World, but a similar dualism appears nationally in the industrialized welfare states. The rule of law is of more assistance to the business community than to underprivileged groups.

This can be explained quite simply by the fact that those who possess extensive rights have more to gain from mechanisms that protect rights than do those who hope to gain new rights. New rights are established by political means, means that are less accessible to underprivileged groups than to others. In spite of this, marginal groups (the unemployed, the disabled, old people, etc.) have acquired minimum rights in the welfare states. And the establishment of these rights is precisely the criterion that is often used to define the welfare state.[57] Modern West European states are simultaneously welfare states and law states. The welfare state may favour underprivileged groups, while the law state favours those with privileges. These rights are not balanced in such a way as to create equality. Inequalities persist, albeit on a higher level than in the old law state.[58]

We shall have occasion, in chapter 7, to return to the problems associated with rule of law doctrines as they appear in current pronouncements on human rights.

Notes

1 A. V. Dicey, *Introduction to the Study of the Law of the Constitution* (London: Macmillan, 1968), p. 188.
2 ibid., p. 193.
3 See Carl Joachim Friedrich, *Man and his Government* (New York/San Francisco/Toronto/London: McGraw-Hill, 1963), pp. 439–40.
4 A. L. Wade, *Administrative Law* (Oxford: Clarendon Press, 1977), p. 23.

5 ibid., p. 23.
6 ibid., p. 25.
7 Georg Jellinek, *Allgemeine Staatslehre* (Berlin: O. Häring, 1900), p. 333.
8 Helmut Coing, *Grundzüge der Rechtsphilosophie* (Berlin: Walter de Grutzer, 1950), pp. 211ff.
9 *Handwörterbuch der Sozialwissenschaften,* vol. 8. (Stuttgart: Gustav Fischer; Tübingen, J. C. B. Mohr (Paul Siebeck); Göttingen, Vandenhoech & Ruprecht, 1964), pp. 768–9.
10 Johs. Andenæs, *Grunnlov og rettssikkerhet* (The Constitution and the Rule of Law) (Bergen: Chr. Michelsens Institutt, 1945), p. 5.
11 Frede Castberg, *Forelesninger over rettsfilosofi* (Lectures on Legal Philosophy) (Oslo: Universitetsforlaget, 1965), p. 180.
12 Torstein Eckhoff, *Forvaltningsrett* (Administrative Law) (Oslo: Tanum-Norli, 1978), p. 87.
13 ibid., p. 90.
14 Johs. Andenæs, *Statsforfatningen i Norge* (The Constitution of Norway), 4th edn. (Oslo: Universitetsforlaget, 1976), p. 170.
15 Geoffrey Marshall, 'Notes on the rule of equal law', in J. Roland Penmoch and John W. Chapman (eds.), *Equality. Nomos IX* (New York: Atherton Press, 1967), pp. 261–76, esp. p. 263.
16 Friedrich, *Man and his Government,* p. 440.
17 ibid., p. 442.
18 Philip Selznick, with the collaboration of Philippe Nonet and Howard M. Vollmer, *Law, Society and Industrial Justice* (New York: Russell Sage Foundation, 1969), p. 11.
19 ibid., p. 11.
20 ibid., p. 12.
21 ibid., p. 13.
22 ibid., p. 12.
23 ibid., p. 13.
24 ibid., p. 15.
25 ibid., p. 16.
26 Roberto Mangabeira Unger, *Law in Modern Society* (New York: Free Press, 1976), pp. 48ff.
27 ibid., p. 53.
28 ibid., pp. 66ff.
29 Wolfgang Friedmann, *Legal Theory,* 5th edn. (London: Stevens & Sons, 1967). p. 163.
30 *The Dynamic Aspects of the Rule of Law in the Modern Age* (Geneva: International Commission of Jurists, 1965), p. 14.
31 ibid., p. 15.
32 ibid., p. 32; cf. also Mangabeira Unger, *Law in Modern Society,* pp. 86ff.
33 René David and John E. C. Brierley, *Major Legal Systems in the World Today,* 2nd edn. (London: Stevens & Sons, 1978), pp. 193ff.
34 Selznick, *Law, Society and Industrial Justice,* p. 18.
35 David and Brierley, *Major Legal Systems in the World Today,* pp. 200ff.
36 A concept taken from the theory of games. It refers to the wish to reduce to a minimum the risk of a maximal loss. Cf. Morton D. Davis, *Game Theory: a Nontechnical Introduction* (New York/London: Basic Books, 1970), pp. 6, 38–42.
37 Jerome Frank, *Law and the Modern Mind,* 6th edn. (New York: Coward-McCann; London: Stevens & Sons, 1949).
38 Friedrich, *Man and his Government,* p. 434.

39 Adam Smith, *An Inquiry into the Nature and Causes of the Wealth of Nations* (1776).
40 Johan Huizinga, *Homo Ludens* (Boston: Beacon Press, 1955).
41 Alf Ross, *On Law and Justice* (London: Stevens & Sons, 1958), pp. 11ff.
42 Lon L. Fuller, *The Morality of Law* (New Haven/London: Yale University Press, 1964), pp. 5ff.
43 Georg Jellinek, *Die Sozialetische Bedeutung von Recht, Unrecht und Strafe* (Vienna: Alfred Holder, 1878), p. 42.
44 ibid., p. 48.
45 Anders Sandøe Ørsted, Supplement to *Nörregaard, Forelaesninger over den Danske og Norske private Ret* (Lectures on the Danish and Norwegian Civil Law), vol. 1. (Copenhagen, 1804), p. 45.
46 Niccolo Machiavelli, *The Prince* (New York: Mentor Books, 1952), p. 98.
47 ibid., p. 97.
48 Jeremy Bentham, *A Fragment of Government and an Introduction to the Principles of Morals and Legislation,* ed. Wilfred Harrison (Oxford: Basil Blackwell, 1948), p. 189.
49 ibid., p. 415.
50 William Blackstone, *Commentaries on the Laws of England,* 2nd edn. (London: John Murray, 1847), vol. 1, p. 47. (First published 1765.)
51 L. Nørregaard, *Forelæsninger over den Danske og Norske Private Ret* (Lectures on the Danish and Norwegian Civil Law) (Copenhagen: 1784), p. 34.
52 Richard D. Schwartz, and Sonya Orleans, 'On legal sanctions', in Michael Barkun, *Law and the Social System* (New York: Lieber-Atherton, 1973), pp. 63–94, quotation p. 63.
53 ibid., pp. 69–70. Cf. also Lawrence M. Friedman, and Stuart Macauly, *Law and the Behavioral Sciences,* 2nd edn. (Indianapolis/New York: Bobbs-Merrill, 1977), pp. 341–4.
54 James Willard Hurst, *Law and Social Process in United States History* (Ann Arbor, Mich.: University of Michigan Press, 1960), pp. 99ff.; Charles A. Reich, 'The new property'. *Yale Journal,* 73 (1964), p. 733. See also Robert S. Summers, 'The technique element of law'. *California Law Review,* 59 (1971), pp. 39–41.
55 Nils Christie, 'De fratagbare goder' (Alienable Goods), in *Som folk flest* (Like Everybody Else) (Oslo: Universitetsforlaget, 1978), pp. 84–94.
56 C. B. Macpherson, *The Political Theory of Possessive Individualism* (Oxford: Clarendon Press, 1962).
57 Asa Briggs, 'The welfare state in historical perspective', *Archives Européennes de Sociologie,* 2 (1961), pp.
58 A recent Norwegian study elucidated the relationship between established economic rights, centred on property, and the efforts to create new legal instruments aimed at the control of the Civil Service and its administrative decisions. The driving force behind the reforms, under the banner of the rule of law, were representatives of the business community accompanied by members of the legal profession. See Ragnhild Øvrelid, 'Forvaltningen og almenheten' (The Civil Service and the public), unpublished manuscript (Oslo: 1981).

CHAPTER 3

Law and conflicts

In the preceding chapters emphasis has been placed upon possible conflicts between the interests of the state and those of citizens. Such conflicts are implied by the coercive element in definitions of law, as well as in the doctrine of the rule of law and its demand for protection against arbitrary exertion of state power. From both of these points of view, the courts emerge as a focal institution. It is through the courts that the violence of the state may legitimately be released against the individual, and it is through access to the courts that the individual may obtain protection against the state.

However, it is hardly through the fulfilment of these functions that the courts have developed and acquired the specific techniques that characterize their mode of handling the problems that they confront. I believe that these techniques can be understood only if we study interpersonal conflicts and the way in which these may call for intervention by third parties. In the concept of the third party lies an important key to an understanding of the operation of the courts and their less developed predecessors or functional equivalents.

It is not my intention to present a theory of how modern courts, legal techniques and modes of thinking have evolved historically. The approach, rather will be to examine some general features that emerge when two parties are in dispute in circumstances in which an amicable solution is hard or impossible to find. Such situations are part of our everyday experience as human beings and members of society. They are also well documented in an enormously comprehensive and varied literature on conflicts and conflict resolution in many different social and cultural settings.

Ethnographic descriptions of dispute settlement

From the ethnographic or social anthropological literature on conflicts and modes of handling them we may extract some examples that illustrate the status and function of third parties. No claim is made that these examples represent a chronological or evolutionary trend. Some of the studies are illuminating, however, because they refer to somewhat simpler social settings than those we meet in a modern industrial or post-industrial society. We encounter in them situations and institutions that have emerged without the paraphernalia of academically construed theories of law; yet close parallels to these institutions can also be found in operation in our economically advanced societies both within the legal orbit and (perhaps even more) outside it, in the shape of mediation, arbitration or informal group processes.

Hoebel has shown how the third party has been introduced in different forms in a number of primitive tribes.[1] Where law is least developed, this third party is vaguely defined, has little special authority and can function only when invited by the parties to do so. Among the Eskimo it was frequently only the whole community that functioned, rather vaguely, as a mediator or judge — for example, when acting as audience to the song and drum contests that took place between parties in dispute. In some cases a blood feud was prevented by society's demand that a relative of the murderer should execute the act of revenge. This overlap in group membership would serve the same function as the intervention of a third party who enjoyed the confidence of both of the conflicting parties. In general, however, the triadic situation in cases of conflict was very poorly developed in most Eskimo tribes.

Among the Ifugao of Luzon the intervention of third parties in litigation has become more firmly institutionalized. There is no superior governmental agency with independent resources of power and sanctions. The parties to a conflict are required by the norms of society to utilize a go-between, who is not a civil servant, a full time expert or a judge but someone with status and power who may draw upon the resources of his kinfolk in case of need. Normally, conflicts are settled through the go-between's ability to whittle down the claims on both sides until a basis for peaceful settlement is attained. The reason why this so often succeeds must be due in no small part to the fact that if one of the parties rejects the procedural norms or is intransigent, he faces an alliance of his opponent, the go-between and their families. This usually means having to fight against an overpowering enemy, with no practicable way of winning the suit. Hoebel's analysis of Ifugao law offers one of the most clear-cut demonstrations of the functions of triadic arrangements *as such,* because the third person need not be more powerful or more highly qualified than the parties to the conflict.

This is not the case if we examine Hoebel's discussion of the Cheyenne, among whom political authority is institutionalized and invested with its own resources of power and sanctions. The settlement of disputes falls within the province of the chief and the council of headmen. These offices do not constitute specialized judgeships but comprise diverse functions. It is clear, however, that the existence of a specifically legal element in the social structure of the Cheyenne is linked with the existence of third persons who will intervene in conflicts on their own initiative or after being invited to do so.

More explicitly, Gulliver has called for two models or ideal types as a theoretical framework for the interpretation of empirical cases of dispute settlement:

> In the study of the actual processes of dispute settlement we should, I think, as a first step distinguish at least two structurally different modes. One is dispute settlement by *negotiation* between the disputants, each assisted by socially relevant supporters, representatives and spokesmen. Each party seeks to exert what strength it can against the other, such strength ranging from forensic argument and skill to the threat of physical force, from moral pressures to offers or denials of other advantages. Here the result, the settlement, is in effect some mutually acceptable, tolerable resolution of the matter in dispute, based on the assessed or demonstrated strengths of the parties. It is useful to distinguish further between straight negotiations between the two parties and negotiations mediated by some third party or one who is a member of both parties, who has no ability to issue any binding decisions.
>
> The second mode of dispute settlement is by *adjudication,* where a binding decision is given by a third party with a degree of authority. Such a decision is in some way coercive in that the adjudicator (judge or the like) has not only both the right and obligation to reach and enunciate a decision but also power to enforce it. The ability to enforce may range from the virtually absolute to little more than the effective public

expression of accepted norms and standards of expectations in their application to the particular dispute. Authority in whatever degree is commonly reinforced to a greater or lesser extent by the additional pressures of diplomatic persuasion, inducement, moral stricture and appeal to the supernatural.

Essentially the difference is between judgment by an authorized third party, on the one hand, and negotiated agreement without judgment, on the other; that is, the difference between the presence or absence of overriding authority.[2]

This overriding authority is present in modern nation states and has been so in other, more archaic, societies. However, in many so-called primitive, tribal or small-scale societies such authority is weak or missing altogether. Thus, the ethnographic literature abounds with examples of negotiated settlements as the typical method of terminating a dispute. On the basis of fieldwork among the Ndendeuli of southern Tanzania, Gulliver presents his findings on dispute settlement in this community as they occur within the arena of a 'moot' (a meeting of villagers):

In conclusion, the settlement of an intracommunity dispute among the Ndendeuli has these characteristics:

(1) It is typically some kind of negotiated compromise between conflicting claims. Even where a principal's claim is very strong and the balance of bargaining power lies with him, he commonly makes some effort to show tolerance and good will by giving way to his opponent in at least some small degree. Where the balance of bargaining power is less one-sided, compromise is a matter of necessity if settlement is to be made.

(2) It is dependent not only on ideas of norms, rights and expectations and on the respective bargaining strength of both principals and their supporters, but also on considerations of its effects on other men's interests and the continuance of neighbourly co-operation and concord.

(3) It is, and must be, an agreed settlement, accepted by both principals as the best that can be obtained in the circumstances. Ultimately a principal cannot be compelled to accept an imposed settlement, for there is no means of enforcing it. Strong pressures from his opponent's side, from mediators and, if necessary, even from his own side are brought to persuade him to acceptance and agreement. Only by his agreement can the settlement be put into effect and made good.

(4) It is put into effect immediately if at all possible. The compensation or debt is paid, the apology made, the claim renounced, all in the moot. Although not invariably so, a settlement that is not acted upon straight away may be no settlement at all, for the whole dispute may have to be renegotiated at a later date, when the claim is actively exerted again. An

agreement, say to pay compensation later on, may be an ephermal success for one principal but perhaps a more practical success for his opponent; that is, the settlement is really an avoidance of settlement, or an agreement to differ. But it may even be one that in effect is in favor of the defendant. Further, by the immediate completion of a settlement it is hoped to remove the dispute altogether and thus allow for the re-establishment of continued working neighbourly relations.

With the exception, at least sometimes, of (4), these characteristics are probably common to all processes of dispute settlement by negotiation without courts in all societies, including the many kinds in Western industrial societies.[3]

We are here faced with a counter-example to the operation of the modern courts. The prevalence of processes of dispute settlement similar to those described by Gulliver, and the absence of court-like procedures, must be understood against the background of the types of society within which they take place. One particularly relevant characteristic of these societies has been highlighted by Gluckman:

In more differentiated societies a person is linked to a variety of different persons, with many of whom his relationship is formally confined to a single interest, as, for example, that of a labourer with his employer, a bus traveller with the conductor, a housewife with a shopkeeper, even an invalid with a doctor or a churchgoer with a priest. It is chiefly in our simple family that we find the mixed ties that are typical of Barotse society. There nearly every social relationship serves many interests. Men live in villages with their kinsmen or quasi-kinsmen, and by virtue of kinship ties they acquire their rights and obligations. With his kin a man holds land and chattels; he produces goods in co-operation with them and shares with them in consuming these; he depends on them for insurance against famine, illness, and old age; he forms with them religious communities tending the same ancestors; they are responsible for the main part of his education; he seeks his recreation with them.[4]

As suggested by the quotation from Gluckman, in Western societies, and also more generally, there has been a move away from the prevalence of such multiplex social relationships. To a large extent these have been supplanted by one-sided, specialized or simplex relationships. Because of the general trend away from a subsistence to a money economy and the increasing division of labour, the social basis of that kind of dispute settlement *as the single form of law* is being eroded. There may be two especially important reasons for this change. One is that an overriding authority, in the form of the nation-state has been, or is being, established. Another reason is that dependence upon a continuation of social relationships after the dispute settlement is decreasing in many legally regulated areas.[5]

Models and hypothesis

After this brief glance at processes of dispute settlement in small-scale societies, we shall pursue the confrontation of the two models indicated by the concepts of negotiation and adjudication. I hope to demonstrate that the introduction and consolidation of the third party has consequences for the way in which the participants in the process, as well as the audience, may come to conceptualize and reason about conflicts and the proper way of handling them. The hypothesis is that the development of legal thought is a concomitant of the intervention of a third party, and the more so the stronger and more independent this agency is. What characterizes legal thought in its more advanced form will be further specified in the next chapter.

In order to go about the task we have set ourselves, it is necessary to develop a typology of conflicts and of the channelling and processing of disputes. One type is the conflict of interests; the other may be termed dissensus (e.g. disagreement over facts and/or values). These are ideal types, useful for analytical purposes but not intended to constitute two categories between which empirical cases may be neatly distributed. In its simplest form the hypothesis may be formulated thus: conflicts of interest may often lend themselves to settlement by negotiation within a dyadic arrangement. Dissensus may be harder to settle by negotiation and will often demand some kind of triadic structure for settlement. However, the form of a conflict and the way in which a dispute is processed depends also upon the kind of institutionalized mechanisms that are available for the handling of disputes. Thus, the availability of courts may, by their very existence, encourage or even force parties to formulate their troubles in terms of a disagreement over facts and/or norms, notwithstanding the fact that the origin of the conflict reflects simply a clash of interests. Now it is necessary to be more specific about the meaning of our terms.

Conflicts

A conflict, for the purposes of our argument, is a condition of the relationship between two or more individuals, who may also be represented by spokesmen or counsel. In order for a conflict to be present, at least one of the parties must have carried out or planned actions that are bound to harm the other party. The conflict either consists in an objective relationship (the furthering of the interests of one party at the expense of the interests of the other) or it is subjectively expressed through hostility. The subjective and the objective element may be mingled, but they may also be independent of each other. Certain types of competition and contest may cause harm to one party or may provoke frustration even if there is no hostility between the contestants. On the other hand, a party may give vent to strong feelings of animosity or hatred without concomitant objective damage.

Conflicts of interest

A conflict of interest between two actors stems from a situation of scarcity. Both want the 'same thing', but there is not enough of it available for each to have what he wants. In this general sense the basis for a conflict is present in all trading transactions. The seller would like to have more money than the buyer is willing to part with, or he would like to withhold a quantity of the produce that the buyer wants to acquire. This conflict potential is eliminated through the operation of the market, usually so smoothly that no overt signs of conflict appear. If a conflict develops, the solution will often be a compromise. Each party concedes to the reduction of his demands until an agreement is reached, although each possibly continues to believe that he is contributing too much. This agreement is, therefore, not to be interpreted as an ethical commitment to the price as an expression of the just terms of exchange. It is merely to be interpreted as an expression of what the parties find it in their own interests to do, given market conditions.

The opposing interests have been brought together because of a wish to minimize the likelihood of maximal loss on both sides. For the buyer not to buy at all, and for the seller not to sell at all, is often the gravest contingency. Therefore they will be prepared to make considerable compromises in relation to their own real preferences. More important, they will compromise with what they consider to be the just terms of exchange. It is a type of social interaction in which solutions appear to be reached by discouraging the actors from becoming morally involved in a major aspect of the interaction, the condition being that their interests are not diametrically opposed. The gain of one party is not wholly the loss of the other.

The possibilities for avoiding conflicts by this method are sharply reduced when new and destructive incidents affect the relationship. If the contribution that one of the parties has undertaken to make disappears after the interaction has begun but before the exchange is completed, a conflict may arise. Let us say that a car dealer leaves a car that he has sold outside the house of the buyer, but the car, which was locked, vanishes before the buyer comes home. Is he still obliged to pay for the car or not? In such a case, and in the absence of law, one party would have no interest in making any compromise at all. There is nothing that the car dealer needs to obtain from the other party. His gain is the car owner's loss. Since he will hardly receive any contribution from the other in the future, he is not concerned with trying to motivate his behaviour, but is interested solely in terminating the interaction. Were there no law and no force in society, those who wanted to terminate interactions would have all the cards in their hands when transactions went wrong and the issue was no longer the sharing of goods but the sharing of losses. Society, however, has been unwilling to accept that in the case of mishaps of this kind whoever physically possesses the undestroyed part of an exchange should always determine the solution to conflicts about the sharing of a loss.

The way in which society, through law, solves conflicts of interest is such that the parties will often find it advantageous to pursue a negotiation in a spirit of compromise. The legal solution, in common with the solution that accident, fate or ill will may offer to a transaction, tends to ignore the mini-max principle and gives all to one party. But it is typical of many such cases that although one of the parties may stand to gain by rejecting compromise, it is not certain which party it will be. Therefore the one who wants to be sure that he will not lose everything will also make some compromise in conflicts over transactions with which something has gone wrong. We shall deal later with the problem of why legal solutions have this all-or-nothing character, and why it is that some people prefer such solutions in spite of cogent reasons for avoiding maximum loss. The first problem is the question of how courts operate; the second, why anyone should want to make use of them.

Dissensus

Competing or contrasting interests do not in themselves imply disagreement between the parties concerning values. It may even be claimed that a conflict of interest presupposes consensus at least about the value of the goods that are sought by both parties. Let us assume that the object of the conflict of interest is a position of leadership or a superior rank within a group. Such a conflict can arise only if the contestants agree that incumbency of the position has value. The case of sexual rivalry may be even more to the point. Often the area of consensus is sharply limited. But its very presence as a condition of any interest conflict is significant, as it does, paradoxically, draw together the conflicting parties. In this sense conflicts of interest are less fundamental than certain conflicts over values, which may amount to the mutual denial of membership of the human race. Interest conflicts emphasize the similarity of the contestants, their common needs and aspirations. In this lies, no doubt, one reason why politicians who compete fiercely with each other for office nevertheless often get along very well. It seems as if this particular kind of inverse interplay between interest conflict and value conflict serves as a major brake on the outward and destructive manifestations of both kinds of conflict, for it also works the other way around: a profound conflict of values will tend to keep antagonists apart. They do not value the same things and tend therefore to encounter each other less frequently than would otherwise be the case.

A conflict of value is based upon dissensus concerning the normative status of a social object. In itself there is nothing about dissensus that should goad individuals into attacking each other. Nevertheless, there is no doubt that disagreements over values as well as over facts have often contributed to overt and aggressive conflict behaviour, most blatantly in religious and ideological wars. Such conflict behaviour, however, seems almost always to be accompanied by some conflict of interest that derives from the scarcity of power and authority.

One might ask whether conflicts of values can be avoided in the same fashion as interest conflicts (e.g. by compromise and resignation in relation to what seems the ideal solution). It is no doubt possible to formulate statements that contain some elements of one system of values and some of another. Such compromises are frequently reached in negotiations between organizations who want to substitute co-operation for competition. The terms of exchange are very uncertain in such dealings, however. The scent of the illicit often pervades such dealings: 'One cannot trade in values', 'Ideas are not for sale', 'You can't bargain with the truth', etc. The illicit nature of compromise on the level of values and of empirical truth makes it hard to discuss matters quite candidly, and thereby decreases the chance of reaching a solution. One reason for this, I suppose, is that on the level of dissensus it is hard to tell what is give and what is take. Is the person who gives in on a point of value or fact making a sacrifice or a gain? This is uncertain, because norms are double-edged, making demands upon the self as well as upon others. Consequently, it is difficult to assess compromises of value as exchanges of sacrifices and advantages. Neither are those who negotiate over ideological questions supposed to dispose freely of values. There is no private ownership of values: that would contradict their communal origin. The same is true of scientific truth.

One type of dissensus that often leads to conflict is the one concerned with the application of values and norms. Political feuds often take this form, whatever their basis may be. A accuses his opponent of being responsible for a specific policy that contradicts or subverts some important value, say full employment. The feud may then take on a factual character, turning on the question of whether the target of the accusation actually was responsible for the policy, or whether the policy actually led to unemployment. But it may also take on a purer, ideological character, the politician admitting his responsibility for some unemployment, but maintaining that this was the price one has to pay for achieving a value with higher priority — increased efficiency and higher production. It is especially when questions of factual responsibility, of guilt and merit, become part of value conflicts, and they usually do, that a solution based on compromise becomes so difficult to find. Whether and how they can be solved is, of course, also dependent upon the interrelations between the dissensus and the interests of the parties. For the dissension, which appears to be the immediate basis of hostilities, may in its own turn be derived from, or intermingled with, a conflict of interests.

The scheme of analysis

The scheme of analysis that emerges from the considerations advanced above is rather simple. Sources of conflict are classified in two broad categories, dissensus and competing interests. All conflicts (in our sense) can be traced back to one or the other or to both of these conditions. The conditions may be present, however, without leading to a conflict in the sense of expressed hostility or inflicted frustration. The presence of dissensus and/or competing interests is a necessary, but not a sufficient, condition for the emergence of conflict.

If conflicts move towards a solution they may do so in one of two major ways: through bargaining and compromise, or through law and the application of norms to established facts. In a sense, the former conflict-solving mechanisms presuppose that the conflict should be handled as a conflict of interest, while the latter presuppose that it should be handled as a dissensus over facts or norms, although the underlying opposition of interests may be fully recognized. Thus there is a correspondence between the two sources of conflict and the two mechanisms for its solution, but we have no reason to assume that the source of the conflict alone will determine the mechanism of solution. It is an empirical problem to discover what sources of conflict, lead to what kinds of conflict-solving mechanisms, and under what additional conditions.

Conflicts may be transformed when they pass from the stage of aggravation to the stage of solution, and this may often be dependent upon the availability and effectiveness of the apparatus for conflict resolution. But it may also depend upon other factors. The preceding must not be interpreted to exclude the possibility that conflicts may be terminated without the application of any conscious conflict-solving method. Such cases do not particularly interest us, but a variety of conflict-solving mechanisms, intermediary between law and bargaining, are of great interest. A market price may solve conflicts in a way that is reminiscent of law, as may arbitration, while mediation must be considered a modified type of bargaining.

Law as a conflict-solving mechanism

I shall consider now the possible transformation of conflicts that occur, or have already occurred, when they are handed over to the law. At the same time, certain possible relationships between the nature of legal conflicts and the numerical aspects of the interaction will be suggested.

When a conflict of interests is turned over to the law it must from then on be formulated as a dissensus, a conflict of values or beliefs. It may be that this transformation has already occurred in the heat of the conflict prior to the intervention of lawyers and courts, thus making it insoluble through compromise. But if the transformation has not already occurred, it must take place before the parties can enter into effective litigation. When a conflict turns into a law suit something else is also bound to happen: The basic interaction changes from a dyad to a triad. Between these two transformations there exists a functional relationship.

Let us first see what is implied when a contrast of interests is turned into a dissensus. The clash of interests is formulated from then on as a disagreement either concerning certain facts in the past or concerning which norms apply to the existing state of affairs, or both, so that it is often hard to distinguish clearly between questions of fact and questions of law. The needs of the parties, their wishes for the future, cease to be relevant to the solution, or, at least they become less significant. Whether the solution harmonizes two contrasting sets of needs and plans for the future is no longer a primary consideration. The problem has become objective in the sense that a solution can be reached by an outsider who knows the rules of evidence and is able to perform logical manipulations within a normative structure. By comparing the available facts with the norms, he can reach a verdict. As long as an interest conflict remains pure, no outsider, no third person can arrive at a conclusion on his own. A solution entails the adjustment of needs on both sides.

This suggests one area where law seems superior to the market: it permits third parties to determine in advance (in the abstract) how certain conflicts are to be solved. This is what makes it possible in law to combine the function of creating predictability with the function of solving individual conflicts. Under certain conditions the 'free market' also does that, but only when the objects of the interest conflicts are replaceable or standardized. Otherwise a solution to an interest conflict that is based on the reciprocal adjustment of needs is ill suited to the promotion of predictability. Similarly, the adjustment mechanism leaves out of consideration the fact that the solution that the parties reach may affect the rest of society.

From the point of view of the contestants, the transformation of the conflict from one of interests to one of values and belief imposes certain restrictions. They are no longer free to disregard the past, to let the dead bury their dead. Questions of law can be solved only by determining guilt or innocence or by ruling on whether the factual bases of alleged rights or duties actually exist, whether a contract has actually been signed, whether it does say what it claims to say and so on. In the mutual adjustment of needs in the market the question of what has been said or done before can be left unsettled if it suits the parties. In such negotiations, furthermore, the parties can often (but not always) disregard the precedent implications of the settlement. There is no implication that it must be interpreted as an application of generally valid rules, applicable to similar cases. Obviously, this extends a certain freedom that is absent in the typical legal situation. A bargain struck leaves no mark upon the normative order; it is not a consequence of it, nor does it become a constituent part of it. In this lie both its advantages and its disadvantages.

Society often has a stake in what goes on between two conflicting parties, especially when they have reached the point at which only one will stand to gain in the future by a change of the *status quo.* This is usually the case after a loss, whether the loss is due to an accident, to fraud or negligence, to inability or to a crime. A bargain may still be struck, but there is also a danger that aggression will make for new losses, including the possibility of murder in revenge. The history of many primitive societies, and of some civilized ones, shows that such revenge may exact a heavy toll and may become the concern of people other than the parties involved. As a matter of fact, methods for handling conflicts have evolved so as to ward off such eventualities. They usually consist in the institutionalized intervention of some third party in the dispute. In this lies the embryo of the legal phenomena, and the basic outcome is that the dyad has become a triad.

It is always the case that when a third party intervenes in a conflict between two people, a fresh possibility arises — there may be an alliance.[6] Instead of the stalemate one to one, the conflict may become two to one. One possibility, of course, is that both the two original contestants become antagonistic towards the third person and decide to agree so as not to let the newcomer influence the settlement. This mechanism, bringing conflict partners together in common antipathy to outside interference, operates in many situations, but predominantly where a developed legal or administrative system already exists.[7] For the original crystallization of legal techniques, however, it must have been more significant that the newcomer might join one of the parties, making it unnecessary for him to compromise with the other, now found to be in the wrong.

The formation of an alliance makes it possible, although not necessary, that one side will have to bear all the loss involved in the case — that is, to acquiesce completely to the demands of the other party. Such will rarely be the outcome when there are only two parties, unless the power differential between them is very great. Usually it takes the participation of a third person to enforce a dichotomous view on the rights and wrongs of a case. Only when one person can be defined as 'guilty', 'liable', or 'responsible' does a settlement take on a clear normative meaning. It becomes something more than a settlement between two parties; it is a demonstration of the validity of a rule of behaviour and a statement about past events.

With the third party the norm of objectivity has been institutionalized, although it may well remain unrealized. When two parties meet and reach a settlement on their conflicting interests they do not necessarily have to agree on either norms or facts (although they may), but only on the single point in space and time on which their interests converge. The result is subjective in somewhat the same sense as the 'I—Thou' encounter in Martin Buber's writings.[8] With the third party the original relationship will almost necessarily become objectified as an 'It', subsumable under general norms. One reason why it may have to become objectified in this sense is the marked increase in the difficulty of settling the relationships in a triad simply and without reliance upon general norms. It may be questioned whether the 'I—Thou' method of adjusting opposing interests can be extended beyond the dyad. The introduction of a third person may inevitably imply a change of technique for conflict resolution if settlement is to be reached.[9]

Modes of cognition in the triad

In a triad each of the participants can look upon the relationship of the other two as an object, something to be described and classified. It is not directly experienced, and nothing can be done about it without some conceptualization. Since we are, for the moment, considering the general properties of the triad, irrespective of the qualifications and mode of recruitment of the third person, it may be asked why this conceptualization should tend to be normative and not causal or functional. There is probably nothing inherent in the triad to prevent such a mode of perception of others and of the relationship between the others. The two modes of perception, the normative and the causal,[10] share the requirement of a general classification of the relationship and a grasp of certain past facts. If the third person is recruited to the triad with the explicit purpose of effecting a settlement between the two original members, however, there are good reasons why he will soon abandon a causal—functional approach to their problem. To pursue a causal approach will often mean to attempt to 'cure' the relationship, just as a doctor tries to cure his patient by removing the cause of his trouble. Some 'causes' of an unresolved conflict of interests are easy to perceive (for example one or both of the parties may be greedy, negligent, lazy). These terms indicate that the arbiter of interpersonal conflicts will find it very hard to pursue a causal line of thinking without committing himself to normative judgments. Whenever he looks for causes of interpersonal conflicts, he is likely to find acts that imply responsibility and are open to evaluation in normative terms.

One may raise the question of whether the third party, by virtue of his position, will tend towards the opinion that there must be some wrong on both sides. He can ally himself with one of the parties and can thereby enforce a completely asymmetrical view of responsibility for the conflict, but there may be reasons, intrinsic in the triadic situation, why he should try to avoid this. If he sides completely with one of the contestants, he jeopardizes his status as an outsider to some extent. He sacrifices his unique moral standpoint in the little group. Although his interests differ from those of the other two, in normative terms he becomes one in a sub-group of two. It seems that in terms of power and authority he will generally stand to gain by assuming a position somewhere between the claims of the two parties, possibly maximizing his own moral superiority the nearer the solution lies to the golden mean. If he suggests a middle-of-the-road settlement, he comes out of the conflict as the only one of the three who has taken the normatively correct position. The other two have presented themselves as extremists, having exaggerated the importance of this or that point or having somewhat misrepresented the facts.

It is precisely in outcomes of this sort that we can see one of the attractions of letting oneself be used as a third party, a middleman, a mediator in disputes between others. It affords one the opportunity of enhancing one's prestige by showing oneself to be a little more right than other people who get themselves involved in conflicts that they cannot settle on their own. This tendency may often be overridden by other factors, of course, – by the actual merits of the case, by the opinion of the rest of society, by bribery or particularistic attachments – but as a force it seems to inhere in the triadic situation when it is built on the basis of a dyad in a state of conflict. Through this mechanism the triadic situation may settle the conflict at very much the same point as the one at which the two parties would have converged if they had been able and willing to carry on with their own bargaining and adjustment. To the interests of the two in reaching a compromise is added the interest of the third person in keeping his 'unique' role and avoiding a complete alliance.

In a triad the possibility of such a full normative alliance does exist, however, and in many cases society's interests seem to demand a full alliance, as between the victim of a crime and the prosecution. Nowadays we would say that any inherent tendency of the judicial system to distributing blame evenly between the criminal and his victim is a perversion of justice. This is not objectivity, although objectivity requires that the factual story, as rendered by the victim, should be received as sceptically as that of the defendant. However, the conclusion will usually, but not always, be that the blame rests wholly with one side, even if the court does not side wholeheartedly with the claims of the prosecution.

This view of the relationship between the criminal and the victim does not seem to have been universally dominant. It seems, rather, to be a fairly modern development to look upon the criminal and the victim as belonging to two different and opposing moral spheres of society, the deviants and the law-abiding citizens. The normative asymmetry in the perception of criminals and victims reaches its apex in the notion of the criminal as someone who, without considering his relationship to his victim, can be classified as belonging to a certain type not only in normative but also in causal—genetic terms. Criminality should, then, be amenable to diagnosis without knowledge of any particular conflicts of the kind that is defined as crime.

Such a conception is strikingly different from the notion of crime as we understand it from the Old Norse sagas. The crimes that occurred in Old Norse society were breaches of laws or infringements of other people's rights. But it is characteristic that these crimes are described as elements of feuds, as parts of interpersonal conflicts, unintelligible without detailed knowledge of the history of the individuals and their interrelationships. The most heinous crimes took place in the 'best society', between equals. Like war, they must be regarded as 'diplomacy carried on by other means'. They were indistinguishable from the feuds out of which they arose. Murder was often settled by the payment of compensation, the amount (*wergild*) being agreed upon after bargaining between the siblings of the criminal and his victim. Implicit in this procedure, in which a third party is vaguely discernible, is an assumption that there might be some wrong on both sides.

In the intrinsic tendency of the third party to take a middle-of-the-road view may lie one of the most primitive roots of an hierarchical moral ordering of society. If people in conflict are unable to settle their differences and need a third person's intervention, they can hardly fail to accord him higher status than he has had before. He performs a social service by resolving a stalemate and receives, almost automatically, a kind of moral 'tax' in addition to the economic rewards that he is often given for his services. Still, this tendency may also introduce a bias, since there is no reason why the claims of one party to a conflict should not be predominantly just. Herein lies a cogent reason why the third person should be made independent both of the need for alliance with one of the parties and of the opportunity to enhance his own social position by middle-of-the-roadism: hence the need for social agencies that are sufficiently strong to handle the two conflicting parties, independent of alliances, and whose status is permanently secured in their professional role, independent of the outcome of individual cases.

This is what genuine courts attempt to establish through organs that dispose of resources of power that enable them to solve conflicts without resorting to alliances. The third party is firmly institutionalized, his social status independent of the outcome of any one case. His independence will often be demonstrated through the evening out of decisions in the long run. He may rule in favour of the insurance company in some cases and find for the insured in some others. He may decide in favour of the wife in some divorce cases but in favour of the husband in others.

From what has been said so far there are some indications of how judges will tend to handle legal suits. In the chapter that follows these leads will be pursued through an analysis of the advanced legal style applied by modern Western courts and elaborated upon in legal scholarship. My thesis is that these more detailed characteristics of legal thinking are determined in part by factors that operate in a triadic conflict-solving arrangement; in part they are to be interpreted as a response to those individual needs that seem to find expression in the rule of law doctrine, as specified in chapter 2.

Notes

1 E. Adamson Hoebel, *The Law of Primitive Man* (Cambridge, Mass.: Harvard University Press, 1954).

2 Philip H. Gulliver, 'Introduction to case studies of law in non-Western societies', in Laura Nader (ed.), *Law in Culture and Society* (Chicago: Aldine, 1969), p. 17.

3 Philip H. Gulliver, 'Dispute settlements without courts: the Ndendeuli of southern Tanzania', in Nader, *Law in Culture and Society*, pp. 67–8.

4 Max Gluckman, *The Judicial Process among the Barotse of Northern Rhodesia* (Manchester: Manchester University Press, 1955), pp. 17–18.
5 See Laura Nader and Harvey F. Todd Jr. (eds.), *The Disputing Process — Law in Ten Societies* (New York: Columbia University Press, 1978), pp. 12–13.
6 Kurt H. Wolff (ed.), *The Sociology of Georg Simmel* (Glencoe, Ill.: Free Press 1950), pp. 135ff.
7 Julian Pitt-Rivers, *The People of the Sierra* (Chicago: University of Chicago Press, 1961), pp. 160ff.
8 Will Herberg (ed.), *The Writings of Martin Buber* (New York: Meridian Books, 1956).
9 Theodore Caplow, 'A theory of coalitions in the triad', *American Sociological Review,* 21 (1956), pp. 489–93; Theodore Caplow, *Two Against One. Coalitions in Triads* (Englewood Cliffs, NJ: Prentice-Hall, 1968).
10 Vilhelm Aubert and Sheldon L. Messinger, 'The criminal and the sick', in Aubert, *The Hidden Society* (Totowa, NJ: Bedminster Press, 1965), pp. 25–54.

CHAPTER 4

Legal reasoning

It is possible to characterize an intellectual style, a universe of discourse, only by comparison with others. The same is true of legal reasoning. In their passing references to the characteristics of different methods of adjudication and different legal styles, Selznick and Mangabeira Unger compare them with adjacent 'thoughtways', similarly applicable to human affairs. In the analysis of the differences in the handling of conflicts between dyads and triads, the judicial mode was compared above with the market as a method. Now we shall compare legal reasoning, typified by the judicial style, with methods and 'thoughtways' that are implemented by other types of third party — by administrators, managers or experts. It is natural, for comparative purposes, to choose other disciplines that are associated with problems close to the concerns of lawyers, ranging from medicine to economics and sociology. These disciplines follow, in no small measure, the example set by the natural sciences.

Our comparison must necessarily rest upon some simplification, a schematization, of law as much as the other social sciences; many nuances must be omitted. Significant differences within the group of social sciences, excluding law (for example, those between economics and sociology) will be discussed in chapter 5. The purpose of the comparison of law and the behavioral sciences is not exclusively to detail the contrasts but also to show points of merger, overlap or combination.

Law as an all-encompassing system

An intellectual structure and method that arises in response to a widespread human need and demand for certainty and security must encompass everything. It must, in principle, provide for an answer to any question. Religion has often been conceived of as such a system. On the mundane level, law and its specific ideological components (like the rule of law doctrine) constitute similarly comprehensive intellectual systems. How is this feasible, when we consider the uncertainties so clearly evident in the behavioral sciences, which are swamped by unsolved questions and provide few answers?

One way of formulating and attempting to explain this paradox is to claim that law has a different kind of relationship with the real world than do these other disciplines. Law is a normative science. I would express it somewhat differently: The reason why law can answer all questions, albeit in a specific and restricted way, is that it creates its own reality. It does not permit any problems to be legitimately raised other than those that it can answer. All other questions are legally irrelevant, even if lawyers will have to admit that they are far from insignificant. Lawyers, like others, will often feel, and say, that the fundamental needs for security and protection raise problems and demand remedies that are way beyond the capacities of the legal system. But this does not concern the rule of law.

The answers provided by law are of varying value in relation to the needs that prompt the questions. Many of them (maybe most) are perceived as beside the point and unhelpful. A large group of answers are based upon the general and simple principle that everything that is not expressly forbidden is permitted. However, in most situations of choice the actor would like to hear more than that he is not going to be punished should he choose A in preference to B. He wants to know, for example, how to make an investment that will provide him with dependable and substantial profits. Lawyers can proffer advice only on limited aspects of this problem, even though this is a field with highly developed law. And if we move to the innumerable problems that arise in everyday life, in family and school and at work, the potential contribution of the lawyer will often be negligible.

I shall illustrate the scope of law, as well as its limitations, by an example. In the early 1950s the Norwegian bishop Schjelderup, well-known as a liberal humanist, had voiced serious doubts about whether there was such a thing as eternal damnation in Hell. For this he was violently attacked by the highly influential and very orthodox Protestant theologian Professor Hallesby. Schjelderup felt that this attack jeopardized his position as a bishop of the Norwegian state Church. He raised the question of his relationship to the Church with the Department responsible for religion and education. The Department, in turn asked the foremost constitutional lawyer, the liberal humanist Professor Castberg, for a legal opinion on the issue raised by the debate about Hell.

If a lawyer can answer the question of whether or not there is such a thing as eternal suffering in Hell, then surely it would be hard to find a question that is unanswerable by law. As it must have appeared to a large section of the public, Castberg seemed to express disbelief in eternal punishment in Hell. He gave his support, as I think the Department's Social Democratic Minister expected, to Schjelderup, and it traced a comprehensive and expert line of legal argument.

On closer inspection, however, the reader of the opinion will perceive that the question answered by Castberg was a more limited one. What he maintained, as a legal expert, was that by stating his view on damnation in Hell, Schjelderup had not violated his duties as a bishop of the Norwegian Church. For obvious reasons, Castberg did not undertake a professional investigation of the existence and state of affairs in Hell.

One possible, somewhat free, interpretation of Castberg's view would be that, from a legal point of view, Hell both exists and does not exist. This opinion is of limited use to the sinful believer who is nagged by fear of eternal pain in Hell, but it may be of considerable assistance to liberal theologians who are anxious about whether they can be true to their own convictions and yet remain safely within the broad confines of the Church. It concerns their rights as preachers, the freedom of the pulpit. However one interprets the legal opinion delivered by Castberg, the incident shows that it is possible to terminate or temper a conflict by legal arguments, notwithstanding the fact that the source of the tension may lie in a question as intractable to rational argument as one could possibly imagine.[1]

Law does not answer all questions, but it does have available answers to all the questions that it defines as relevant — that is, to all questions *of law.* This is not the case with the natural and the behavioral sciences. These disciplines are studded with unsolved problems that are recognized as eminently relevant. One might say that in law those problems to which there exists no answer must be defined as insoluble (that is, beyond the scope of the law). This has to be the view of the bench, in particular, since a judge is obliged to reach a decision, and one that is grounded in (positive) law. In the other behavioral disciplines almost the reverse is true. The recognition that there are unsolved, but in principle soluble, problems is the *raison d'être* of the research which goes on within these disciplines.

In law it is difficult to draw a line of demarcation between scholarly work and many types of practice, while such a distinction can easily be made between many types of medical research and the practice of healing. The subject matter, the data, of legal scholarship largely comprises texts produced by colleagues, other jurists. Through the vehicle of legal scholarship the legal profession (in a broad sense) analyses its own work. This provides legal researchers with a well ordered set of data on the protocols of the courts and documents leading up to legislation. This material can be investigated by methods that are relatively precise and dependable, and quite empirical within its own limited field. Whether or not more normative considerations enter into scholarly presentation than is the case in the behavioral sciences is not the most interesting problem. The main problem is the limitation of the data base of 'valid positive law'.

If valid law is understood as consisting of codes, judicial decisions and other conventionally accepted 'sources of law' (*Rechtsquellen*), there is reason to claim that legal scholarship is in possession of methods that may meet the demands stipulated by the rule of law with some success. It can sort out what people are entitled to and what rights and obligations they have. The extent to which the rights become operative in practice, however, raises new questions. We shall return to these. So far I have claimed only that the methods of legal reasoning must be understood, in part, as a theoretical basis for the implementation of the rule of law.

It is still necessary to consider the contribution that legal reasoning can make to the feeling of security and protection among the populace, given the rigorous limitations on its recognition of relevant reality. How much reliance people actually place on the law as a guardian and protector is, of course, an empirical question. There is considerable evidence that among the lay population there are some who harbour scepticism towards the law and the legal profession. However, to the extent that law provides for the allaying of fears and dark premonitions, this has to do with the Janus face or law described in chapter 1. Neither the practising lawyer nor the scholar can rely exclusively on conventional and readily available sources of law. Frequently they must consider such imponderables as are subsumed under the heading of teleological factors – the aim of the law, legal consciousness and 'the nature of the case' (*Die Natur der Sache*). Through these wide-ranging excursions into unmapped territory, law has given the impression that it is a general social science; it has functioned as a premature social science, in many respects a precursor of sociology. Lawyers have operated as general 'experts' on social issues that lie far beyond the boundaries of the sources of law.

Law has provided a screen, a grid, by means of which social problems can be localized and ordered into a system of a Linnean kind, based upon phenotypes, not genotypes. Legal scholarship has presented both a comprehensive order, which stipulates how things ought to be done, and a thorough empirical description of certain texts and the activities of judicial and sometimes other types of legal personnel. Legal terminology frequently hovers between normative and descriptive terminology. In spite of the normative aims and the limitations of the empirical data base, the pronouncements of lawyers and legal scholars nevertheless are often interpreted by their audiences as expert opinions on the actual state of affairs in society. Faith in order and predictability has some basis in the legal 'thoughtways', although it must not be forgotten that most of these are unknown to the general public. As Thurman Arnold has put it, people often know no more than that learned people are seriously preoccupied with the ever finer elaboration of a system providing answers to pressing problems.[2]

On falsification

In one brief sentence, the calling of lawyers is to answer, not to question. In the behavioral sciences the value of the inquiring attitude, the acceptance of uncertainty and the lack of answers to some questions, is built into the very ethics of research. Falsification is a mark of the testability (and thus of the scientific status) of a proposition,[3] often a mark of honour. But falsification, for example by the reversal of a judgment in higher courts, is no mark of honour in law. Law is integrated with politics and public administration more profoundly than are the other behavioral sciences. Law is the exertion of power, not only a means by which to guide public policy. There is also a belief that within medicine, psychology, economics and sociology, not to speak of technology and the natural sciences, the number of useful answers increases the more questions one asks. The acceptance of uncertainty, of trial and error, of acknowledged ignorance, is a *conditio sine qua non* for progress. There appears to be no common basis for a similar faith in progress in relation to legal scholarship.

The problem of falsification in law is closely related to the way in which the law handles the tension between generality and uniqueness in its treatment of cases. The rule of law doctrine calls for predictability, generality and equality. Bills of attainder are condemned; general rules are demanded. In concrete cases before the courts, however, it is not obvious how these notions should be interpreted. Predictability may easily clash with concrete justice.

If a judge were to subsume a case under a rule in a fairly mechanical way, this might appear to furnish the most reliable basis for prediction: if somebody stole goods of a value ranging from £*x* to £*y* by breaking into a house, and if he had a previous record of a certain severity, then the penalty would be so many weeks or months in prison. Given that potential offenders base their predictions upon the records of the trial courts, this kind of taxation system, still practised in traffic cases, would provide for maximum predictability, as well as equality.

Now, for a variety of reasons, this type of system has fallen into disrepute. What is of interest here is that it would be a dubious practice even from the rule of law point of view. It is unlikely that those who are affected by the law base their predictions, or their judgment of what is equal and what is not, exclusively or even predominantly upon those criteria that are stipulated in the legal rules. For many, perhaps the majority, an important basis for such prediction is to be found in the informal norms and values of their social environment, their private and local ethics. From these norms emerge criteria for predictions and comparisons that can modify the conclusions to be drawn from a mechanical reading of a legal rule. The rules themselves may express their elasticity by referring to rather vague behavioural standards or by the leeway given the trial judge in the meting out of punishment.

An obvious example of the clash between two measures of equality is the stipulation of fines. Formal equality, which might foster predictability, would cause unequal amounts of suffering. For a rich man £100 is not much of a burden, while such a fine might create enormous problems for a poor man. Many believe, although I don't, that a brief stay in prison is of no serious consequence to a homeless vagrant, while it is almost catastrophic for a respectable member of the middle class. Even predictions can vary in the case of these 'folk conceptions' and may lead to surprises if the law is followed strictly and applied literally.

Faced with such dilemmas judges use a technique that consists in the more or less skilful blending of the general and the unique. The demands of justice require that emphasis is placed on the clear and generally formulated criteria of the law in the books. However, they also require of the judge a sensitivity to the peculiarities of the case that call other norms and values into operation. This leads to a certain amount of individuation in the decisions of the courts and in judicial opinions.

In an attempt to harmonize the demands for schematic predictability and equality with the demands for concrete justice in the individual case, judges miss or waive the opportunity to make their own – and their colleagues' – future behaviour maximally predictable. The grounds given for verdicts are usually formulated in such a way that cases appear to fall into certain general categories, while at the same time preserving a uniqueness that makes it difficult to compare them with other, similar cases. Strictly speaking, there are no cases that are identical – or if there are, one would have to make an extensive search to find them.

This means that a verdict cannot easily be falsified by future verdicts in similar cases. Inequality before the law may be a reality, but it is hard to prove by reference to statistics as will be shown in chapter 6. The avoidance of falsification may be an additional reason for the choice of this technique in adjudication, of which one aspect is the application of an old principle known as 'Occam's razor': no grounds should be given other than those necessary to reach a conclusion in a particular case. There is a tendency to limit the scope of that which is *res judicata* in the decision. The strength of the tendency varies between countries and courts. The US

Supreme Court may deliver more general opinions in constitutional matters than Scandinavian courts are called upon to do. In any event, the tendency towards individuation and the limitation of the *res judicata* would seem irrational and wasteful within the framework of a natural science or a social science modelled on similar lines. It is a violation of the economy of thought not to use every available opportunity to generalize and build theory. Law is not wholeheartedly dedicated to this as an overriding ideal.

Causality in law

We shall pursue the preceding argument by focusing upon some more specific devices and concepts in law and the behavioral sciences respectively. Causality and the attitude to processes over time provide a starting-point. Law seems to study the causes of actions and their effects in a way that differs from the approach of the behavioral sciences. This is true too of the legal approach to the effects produced by lawyers and judges and by legal enactments of various kinds.

The courts are often faced with the problem of whether or not event A is produced, 'caused', by event B. And it could be claimed that the reasoning of the judges, and especially that of the legislators, is saturated with references to the future consequences of the law and its enforcement. Let us consider first the meaning of causality as it presents itself in the practice of the courts.

The problem of causality appears especially in criminal law and in the law of torts. If someone is charged with liability for someone else's loss, the destruction of something of economic value, the question arises of whether the loss is caused by his actions. In jurisprudence there has been much controversy over the proper meaning of this question.[4] Some have based their argument upon conceptions of causality supposedly derived from the natural sciences. Others have tended towards a normative view, emphasizing the overall reasonableness or unreasonableness of the charge. However, in concrete cases all seem to put the major emphasis upon what a 'reasonable person' could be expected to foresee as a consequence of his action, provided he proceeds with proper caution and care. This means, in effect, that the legal decision-maker and the legal scholar are exempt from undertaking original studies to establish relationships of cause and effect that could not already have been anticipated by laymen involved in the events. Even causal relationships that are fairly well established by science may be considered irrelevant if the individual cannot be regarded as imprudent for not having been aware of them.

However this may be, is it correct that the legal decision-maker never develops into an expert on the kinds of factual relationships that are relevant to the solution of questions of liability and guilt? Usually the relationships are much too varied for that. In some specific areas, however, he may become a well informed layman. Overall the legal profession as such does not work creatively to discover the new causal relationships.

To sum up, it may be said that law is not unconcerned with causal relationships, but their delimitation and sometimes their interpretation are narrowly defined by normative considerations. The function of legal thought in relation to such causal problems is purely passive and receptive. Therefore the usual methods applied in the causal sciences have not profoundly affected the structure of legal thinking and decision-making.

The study of the causation of crime has developed into a separate scientific discipline, clearly distinguishable from criminal law as a branch of legal scholarship. Between the two there is considerable interaction and mutual influence, which have had important consequences in relation to the rule of law. For the criteria, the factors that are prominent in the study of crime causation and of rehabilitation programmes, often coincide with those upon which folk conceptions focus. A broken home, a nervous breakdown in the background may be a cause of crime, but it is also a morally extenuating circumstance. Thus criminology has to some extent functioned as an exercise in a morality beyond, possibly above, the law. Criminology and natural law, in many ways at opposite poles, have areas of mutual relevance, where *les contraires se touchent.*

The difference between criminology and criminal law becomes evident even in their definitions of the common subject matter, criminality. Between the legal and the criminological applications of the concept of crime there are tensions. Criminologists have attempted to develop concepts of crime that capture a genotypical reality. There have been attempts to delimit types of behaviour (for example, 'white-collar crime')[5] on the basis of hypotheses about common causal factors, an endeavour rooted in the quest for generality and economy of thought that is also aimed at prediction. This has led many social or behavioral scientists to lump certain types of criminal together with other types of deviant. In the eyes of psychiatrists, the crime as such recedes into the background, while categories like psychopathic personality or weak super-ego, etc. become dominant. For the sociologist the general category of deviance may take precedence, and crime assumes a subordinate status as a somewhat accidental manifestation of underlying social ills. For a long time criminologists neglected large areas of illegal and punishable activities and concentrated their attention rather narrowly on theft, murder and sexual offences.

The criminal lawyer takes his mandate from the law as it defines punishable acts. The courts deal with theft and drunken driving in the light of the same principles in spite of the substantial differences in causal factors. They emphasize those phenotypical differences that have a normative basis in law, often without any connection with other psychological or social factors. A defendant who stands accused of tax evasion may receive the same penalty as a homeless vagrant who has beaten up his companion, irrespective of the glaring differences in the social causes and implications of the two illegal acts. On the other hand, someone who has omitted important sources of income in his tax declaration and another who is found guilty of embezzlement may receive very different punitive reactions, although the two types of situation may be similar in terms of causation.

In spite of such dissimilarities between the approaches of the criminal lawyer and the criminologist, a rapprochement is taking place. Having chosen this way of presenting his discipline, the criminologist cannot neglect the legal categories. His dependence on criminal statistics, bound by the legal categories, forces him to make use of this scheme of classification. Cumbersome and time-consuming fieldwork and original surveys are required if he wants to work with his own categories. The other side of the coin is that the trial judge and those responsible for penal policy-making now expect to be obliged, and to be able, to consider and take heed of research findings on the causes of crime and the effects of different penalties.

The responsibility of the legal profession, when faced with such problems, is strictly limited. The causal problems involved are often of a very complex nature, as the theories about prevention and deterrence in criminal law show. It seems quite clear that the legal profession is not much engaged in working out the factual relationship between legal decisions and the subsequent psychological state of individuals or the sociological state of social systems. The problems involved do not belong to any one scientific area but cut across many. A lawyer cannot, therefore, easily become an expert on such problems; or if he were to become an expert, he might lose contact with his legal concerns. Even more significant, the judge is not responsible, in the juridical sense, for the verity of the hypotheses he advances concerning the factual consequences of his decisions. There is no institutionalized device that has to verify — or falsify — the consequences of a legal decision once it is out of the hands of legal personnel. If the judge has correctly assessed certain facts that now belong to the past and has correctly subsumed them under a law that he has 'found', he is invulnerable irrespective of what happens in the future. What may cause falsification is future events, the digging up of new evidence, which may show that he was mistaken about the past.

The contrast between the causal construction of reality as a process and legal reasoning becomes very apparent if we compare the legal model of the criminal with the medical model of the sick. I have dealt at some length with this problem in other contexts and refer the reader to these papers.[6] Here I shall follow up one aspect of these comparisons, namely, the handling of time in law and in the causal sciences.

The law and time

The special and marginal relationship with causal explanations is closely associated with the legal approach to time. Natural sciences and many social sciences study processes over time and put great effort into developing predictions about the future course of events. They are out to establish invariant sequences of events along the axis of time, regularities that make it possible to develop hypotheses from which one can derive predictions. Two disciplines as different as medicine and economics are both vitally concerned with the anticipation and control of future events, albeit on different levels.

It is a paradox that law, which promises predictability through its much publicized dedication to the rule of law, is not a predictive science. The structure of law was linked in the preceding chapter with the triadic arrangement and the conditions under which third parties can participate effectively in conflict resolution. In this situation, and in the craving of the parties for certainty and safety, there is pressure in the direction of a legal, not a scientific, mode of decision-making. The wish for predictability leads to a judicial orientation towards the past, to establish what the parties (or the defendant) have done, said and meant. If a judge looks to the future, he must try to take account of as many factors in the situation as he possibly can. If he wants to prognosticate on the basis of a defendant's response to a certain rehabilitation programme and lets this determine his verdict, he will make his own decisions harder to predict than if he used a tariff scheme.

The contrast between law and the behavioural sciences might be expressed in these terms: the behavioural sciences attempt, among other things, to increase predictability in human affairs by discovering causal connections that may furnish a basis for the prediction of a broad spectrum of phenomena. The issue could be someone's state of health two weeks from today or the size and welfare of the population in about the year 2000. Such forecasts are often quite uncertain, sometimes entirely useless, and the interplay between all the factors involved is not well understood.

The contribution that law can make to predictability is of an altogether different kind. It consists in the *creation* of a general myth of predictability with a certain foundation in real legal practice that can be predicted. The cost of this method is that it precludes the opportunity to investigate phenomena other than 'what the courts will do in fact'. It cannot contribute to any increase in forecasting skill outside its own 'jurisdiction'.

I use the term 'myth' because lawyers and the law cannot, in practice, carry out the programme of systemic order that seems to be intended by the rules. There may be an unambiguous proscription against driving at a speed of 80 miles per hour when the limit is 70. The fine for such a transgression may be fixed at £20. Nevertheless, this gives us little information about what will actually happen if we drive at 80 m.p.h. Usually nothing happens, except that we reach our destination a little earlier than if we had abided by the law. What we know with a fair amount of certainty is that if we drive at a speed below 70, we shall not be fined. The rule of law relates to this latter kind of prediction: a guarantee against unlawful interference by the police or other public servants. However, a drastic gap between the law in books and the law in action is of relevance to some aspects of the rule of law, albeit not the most central one. If rules that claim to defend important human interests are violated *en masse* without consequences for the perpetrators, many will experience this as a failure to enforce the rule of law. It is considered very important that murderers be caught so as to confirm the prediction that the crime of murder is extremely likely to lead to judgment and a severe penalty.

When a lawyer studies the consequences of legally operative facts, like contracts, birth, death, damage, illness, crime, qualifying exams, etc., he does not investigate a process over time. This is one of the implications of the normative character of legal reasoning. His task is not to find out what actually happens after these events have taken place. The bond between the event and the consequence is on the level of the 'ought'. The law stipulates what a valid consequence should be, irrespective of what actually happens. Although most families may never experience the calamities that are regulated by the law on divorce, custody, the distribution of property, etc., these rules are valid for these families, as for all others. Rules that are seldom applied do not lose their legal validity if the events which precipitate enforcement rarely occur. Nor does massive hidden criminality challenge the validity of traffic or tax laws.

Legal reasoning is oriented towards the past and treats the succeeding course of events in a discontinuous fashion. When the trial judge today takes a stand on a crime that took place last year, he deals with a discrete action committed at a certain point in time and is normally unconcerned with later events. When he metes out a prison term, he does so primarily with reference to the severity of the offence. Time functions in this respect as fines do, and as bodily mutilation used to, as a measurable amount of inflicted suffering.

However, on this score the pure legal model has been modified and supplemented in recent times by borrowings from the behavioural sciences. Processes over time play their part in attempts to build treatment, education and rehabilitation into sanctions, especially as regards juvenile delinquents. Length of stay in an institution is seen in relation to an expected process of change within a time dimension. The judge may think that a stay in an institution must last for a certain time if any results are to be achieved, or he may believe that a young offender should serve only a brief spell in prison, so as to avoid the possible negative consequences of a longer stay.

The absence of probabilism (stochastic models) in legal reasoning

Predictions of processes over time will usually assume a probabilistic form, appearing as hypotheses about what is likely, but not certain, to happen. Legal reasoning is not couched in this form, although the factual relationship between operative facts and legal consequences are of a stochastic nature. An element of randomness is involved. Modern legislation provides evidence that the relationships have to be of this kind. The law establishes certain general principles or goals but leaves much of their implementation to the discretion of administrative agencies and the courts. Indirectly probabilism has left its mark upon modern legislation through the use of standards and the delegation of regulatory authority to subsidiary bodies.

A legal judgment decides not that something probably happened but that a certain fact must be considered as established or as not established. It does not say that a specific decision is probably right, or that a rule is valid law with a certain degree of probability. The decision is, in the final analysis, either right or wrong; a rule is valid or invalid.

The rules of evidence in law must be understood as arising from a compromise between the wish to find out what has happened and the need to reach a decision that will fit into a normative system with given properties. Legal decisions often have to be reached fairly quickly if they are to serve any purpose at all, or to give other cases a chance to be dealt with. As a result, certain rules have arisen, defining stages in the procedure at which new evidence becomes inadmissible. Quite generally, rules contain certain restrictions on the kinds of evidence that may be introduced in court. It is thus not permissible in a defamation case in a Norwegian court of law to introduce evidence to show that the plaintiff really committed a crime for which he has previously been acquitted.

Court proceedings are, in principle, public. Because of the conflict that takes place before the court, any fact that is brought forward takes on a normative colour. There is no room for pure fact-finding, in the sense in which this is possible in the laboratory, in the privacy of the doctor's consulting room or in the anonymity of the social survey. The question of establishing a fact becomes almost inevitably one of making a fact public and of laying it open to the partisan, normative interpretation of legal counsel, unrestricted by demands for strict objectivity.

Were there no normative constraints upon the search for truth, it would often be impossible to reach any conclusion about what has happened. This is not to deny that an impressive amount of fact-finding goes on in support of the court's verdict. And in many respects the work of the police may conform to high standards of scientific observation. Still, there is often (perhaps usually) room for doubt about the history of a case. Such doubt is, of course, perfectly normal in science, although scientists may sometimes be tempted to forget it. In experimental work it is standard procedure for a researcher to set up a number of competing hypotheses to be tested one by one. Even in historical research several alternative sequences of events may be suggested and their relative probabilities estimated. A legal decision-maker may proceed in a similar manner up to a point, but in the end he will have to decide in favour of a single version of what happened as *the* truth.

This might seem odd, unrealistic and unjust in cases in which there is considerable doubt about the facts, in which it is almost equally probable that the events did and did not take place. In such cases a simple rule to the effect that the most probable version should be the basis of the verdict would not only contradict certain other normative considerations but would also give clear expression to the view that law builds upon probabilities and not upon certainties. In the face of grave doubt there is, of course, no way of denying this. The interesting point, however, is that procedural law, rather than encouraging frank statements about degrees of probability, has devised rules of evidence that tend to obscure the exact degree of uncertainty.

When doubt is considerable, or vaguely qualified, the rules about the burden of proof come into operation. The term seems to indicate that these rules establish the obligation to bring forward evidence, and in a very general way they may possibly tend to encourage one of the parties towards greater activity than the other. But rules about the burden of proof are primarily standards concerning who is to win the case if certain facts remain uncertain beyond a point that may vary but is never clearly defined. The most famous example of this is the principle of criminal procedures *in dubio pro rei.* If there is reasonable doubt about the guilt of the defendant, he is to be acquitted.

Behind this rule lies a normative principle based upon a value consideration: if the court goes wrong on a factual question of guilt, it is better that it should do so in favour of the defendant rather than to his disadvantage. The implication is, however, that if he is acquitted with reference to the rules of evidence, there is no way of inferring from the sentence just how probable or improbable it is that the defendant has committed the crime of which he is accused. From the court proceedings the audience and the public may be able to form their own opinion. But the court will be mute on this question. From the point of view of the law, the defendant has not committed the crime. If somebody accuses him of it later, it will be taken by the court as *res judicata*; it will be deemed that he has not committed it. But the existence of rules of evidence, among them the rules concerning the burden of proof, serve notice that such an assertion is not of the same order as a historian's claim that someone did or did not do something.

The unhampered search for 'probable truth' has, to some extent, been substituted in law by the game of evidence. The outcome is interpreted as bearing upon a world of facts, but it does not essay at all points to maximize realism. This aspect of court proceedings is much clearer in primitive or archaic systems of law. In some cases a genuine game of chance was employed by the court to determine questions of guilt. Trial by ordeal was of this order.[7] Other devices may lack the element of chance but still substitute the formal laying of evidence for an unbounded search for truth (e.g. by the significance attached to the oath taken by witnesses). Modern procedural law seems more scientific, but at some important points it indicates a departure from science that is significant and suggests important differences between the functions of legal decisions on the one hand and of applied science on the other.

Considering the difficulties that are encountered by any science that deals with human affairs when attempting to establish facts, it is fairly clear that a system of legal decision-making that tried to follow the canons of scientific method with utmost consistency would be unable to furnish definitive decisions whenever they were required. Small wonder, then, that legal systems have tried to develop alternative methods, ranging from trial by ordeal to rules about the burden of proof. They fulfil the needs of the judge's most basic task – to reach a decision no matter how great the obstacles may seem. And the need to adopt substitute methods in establishing facts in cases where there is considerable doubt has led to the denial of the probabilism involved.

The other aspect of non-probabilism in law is statements of valid law (e.g. questions concerning rules). The construction of rules in law is achieved by complex methods: the interpretation of codes, the consideration of precedents, the perusal of scholarly opinions, speculations about the functions of the rules. Whatever the 'sources of law' may be, their interpretation is usually beset with doubt.

The uncertainties can be seen clearly both in judicial opinions and in scholarly treatises. They may derive from various sources and may be interpreted as doubts concerning what the courts will probably do, or concerning what they ought to do.

Legal scholarship does not, as a rule, distinguish clearly between the normative and the predictive aspect of such doubts. The aim of both scholars and decision-makers is to arrive in the end at a conclusion that takes the form 'X is a valid rule of law.' Admittedly, this conclusion may be tempered, especially in scholarly work, by qualifying statements to the effect that the interpretation is open to doubt, but it seems that legal thinking tries with all its might to avoid the conclusion that rules X and Y have about equal probability of being valid. This would violate widespread notions concerning the nature of law as certain and predictable and would also, of course, make it difficult for the courts to perform their practical tasks.

The tendency to dichotomize

Legal thinking is thinking in terms of rights and obligations. The tendency in judicial decisions and in legal scholarship is to treat these rights and obligations in a dichotomous fashion. This tendency means that the courts usually find that a person either does or does not have a right or a duty. It may well be that non-probabilism is a necessary condition for this state of affairs to obtain, but it is certainly not a sufficient one. It is logically and morally possible to be quite dogmatic about what has happened and still to decide that the benefits and burdens of these past events should be equally distributed between contesting parties.

To say that legal decisions are based upon a dichotomous mode of thinking about rights and duties does not imply that a court has to side completely with one party to a dispute, although it may sometimes do so. What is implied is that the legal decision-maker works on each separate problem on the basis of a logical model in which persons either have or do not have rights. There is no such thing as a single right belonging only partly to a person. This is not to say that no partial rights exist — but here their partial nature is defined as an intrinsic characteristic of the rights themselves. And since the courts usually have to make several separate decisions, the dichotomous nature of each verdict can be tempered; qualms about conceding that a person is completely right on one issue can be modified by deciding another issue in such a way as to steer the consequences in the direction of a compromise solution.

In tort cases there may sometimes be doubt about the degree of fault of the person who has caused the damage. Nevertheless, the court may decide that he is liable to pay full compensation. It cannot find that, in view of the circumstances and their moral implications, it is unreasonable to make him pay full compensation as well as to exempt him from any liability at all. It cannot state that the right solution is to keep to the middle of the road. The court must find him liable, without further qualification.

But in its decision about the often very complicated problem of what full damages amount to the court may let itself be influenced by lingering doubts about its previous finding. And in practice it may arrive at a compromise by awarding low damages. Whether this procedure is in accordance with law in the strict sense is doubtful, but it has been shown that the principle of compromise is in practice adopted by some courts. And no one would deny, I imagine, that the complexities of legal matters leave considerable room for adjustments of this kind. These adjustments are, however, usually reached without violation of the dichotomous structuring of rights and obligations. A method available to the court for tempering overly one-sided decisions is to use its powers to distribute legal costs between the parties.

In criminal law strictly dichotomous thinking sometimes breaks down. Under the rules about defence and retaliation the law allows for explicit recognition that there may be some right and some wrong on both sides: the offender is guilty, but the behaviour of the victim was so provocative that, to a greater or lesser degree, it mitigates the guilt of the offender. The whole theory of extenuating circumstances can be seen as an important deviation from the pattern of dichotomous thinking that usually prevails when judges or legal scholars deal with the rights and obligations of citizens and public agencies. Nevertheless, even when such considerations enter into the deliberations before the judge, he shall in the end have to decide in terms of guilt or innocence.

There is a paradox, associated with the demand for the rule of law and the need for security, in the either–or character of judicial decisions. Litigation is risky. One of the parties may suffer loss on all counts and may have to pay legal costs as well. Through negotiation, or mediation, a compromise solution might have been reached that would have been preferable, at least for one of the parties. Therefore those who seek security and want to minimize risk will often opt for negotiation and will avoid litigation. In this we can perceive possible tension between predictability and security in disputes.

Predictability provides security and comfort for those who are in a position to comply with existing rules. In many areas of life (e.g. in certain types of business) rigid obedience to the law may entail great difficulties or sacrifice. A certain amount of transgression is normal. Especially when a legal suit is being considered, it is somewhat uncertain on whose side the law finds itself. The parties, motivated by the wish to avoid maximal loss (the mini-max principle) will prefer a settlement out of court, usually based on a compromise. Thus the adjudicative mode of settling disputes, originating in demands for safety and security, can appear risky when a legal suit becomes an imminent reality.

Another paradox should also be mentioned; it is related to the assumption that complete conformity with the demands of the law may be rare and transgressions frequent. This has to do with the emphasis upon the drawing of sharp demarcation lines (for example, between lawful and forbidden behaviour) as a legal technique. These borderlines often lack a moral counterpart; they are somewhat arbitrary, leaving a grey zone on both sides where uncertainty prevails with respect to right and wrong. In certain political systems this situation has been exploited by gathering information about relatively insignificant deviations from the law, not out of a concern to uphold these rules, but as impeccable legal ammunition against people who deviate against more diffuse political standards of acceptable behaviour. A legal technique shaped by the rule of law doctrine becomes a political weapon in violation of the rule of law.

The uniformity and traditionalism of legal concepts

We have discussed the difference between legal and criminological concepts. Usually, legal concepts are more precise, but at the same time they are more conservative, less amenable to change. The scope of concepts such as sale, theft, mortgage ought to be identically, or at least similarly, conceived by everybody, certainly by lawyers. Legal scholarship cannot legitimately introduce new definitions of old concepts, motivated by the scholar's own conception of fruitfulness and other research considerations. If he wants to further change, he has to do so more or less imperceptibly and on a moderate scale. Even the legislator will often find it hard to change the meaning of concepts, because of the systemic coherence of the law and the demand for consistency. Change in concepts of any importance will have repercussions in other parts of the system. Inertia is a characteristic of the law.

The behavioural sciences are different. They are not exposed to the same pressure to be consistent and uniform in their use of terminology. In many fields one can find a rich and varied flora of definitions and terminological use, determined by each researcher's view of how phenomena ought to be classified and described. A conventionalist philosophy has supported this tendency, combined with a cult of originality, which is absent from law. If concepts don't spring automatically from the phenomena themselves, the scientist may feel relatively free to propose new concepts, which is to do no more than challenge conventions without definitive authoritative backing. The problem is almost the opposite of that found in law – there is a plethora of ever-changing terms. Even should this somewhat anomic state in the social sciences be overcome, revision and changes in concepts will continue to occur more frequently, and for different reasons, than in the law.

Wide minimal consensus, the absence of threatening opposition, is a basis for the continued operation of law. Reliance upon tradition becomes inevitable. Against the traditional concepts and rules stand competing, innovative alternatives. Often none of these can gain universal, or even widespread, acceptance. Thus tradition predominates throughout *die normative Kraft des Faktischen.* A mini-max demand for stability and order prevails.

Notes

1 Frede Castberg, *Statsreligion og kirkestyre* (State Religion and Church Governance) (Oslo: Forlaget Land og Kirke, 1954). See also Frede Castberg, *Minner om politikk og vitenskap fra årene 1900–1970* (Memoirs of Politics and Science between the Years 1900–1970) (Oslo/Bergen/Tromsø: Universitetsforlaget, 1971), pp. 260–3.

2 Thurman W. Arnold, *The Symbols of Government* (New Haven: Yale University Press, 1935), p. 70.

3 Karl Popper, *The Logic of Scientific Discovery* (London: Hutchinson, 1959), pp. 78–92; Michael Polanyi, *Personal Knowledge* (Chicago: University of Chicago Press, 1958), pp. 120ff., 177, 309ff.

4 H. L. A. Hart and A. M. Honoré, *Causation in the Law* (Oxford: Oxford University Press, 1959).

5 Edwin H. Sutherland, *White Collar Crime* (New York: Dryden Press, 1949); Vilhelm Aubert, 'White-collar crime and social structure', *American Journal of Sociology,* 58 (1952), pp. 263–71.

6 Cf. Vilhelm Aubert and Sheldon L. Messinger, 'The criminal and the sick', in Vilhelm Aubert, *The Hidden Society* (Totowa, NJ: Bedminster Press, 1965), pp. 25–54; Vilhelm Aubert, 'Legal justice and mental health', *Psychiatry,* 21 (1958), pp. 101–13.

7 See Hermann Nottarp, *Gottesurteile. Eine Phase im Rechtsleben der Völker* (Bamberger Verlagshaus Meisenbach, 1949).

CHAPTER 5

Sociology, law and the sociology of law

In the preceding chapter legal thinking and scholarship were confronted with a contrasting model of analysis. However, this model was rather abstract, presenting no more than fragmented features that play a prominent part in certain branches of science, including some of the social sciences. The rationale for building this model was to throw light upon the characteristics of law as a way of handling and thinking about problems and their solution. A 'dummy' constructed for this purpose cannot do justice to the variety of empirical and analytical styles within the social sciences. It does not mirror faithfully the varieties of sociological thought, for example. In this chapter I shall deal more specifically with the relationship between sociology and law, both in terms of a comparison and by offering some comments on the interplay between law and sociology in the emerging discipline of sociology of law.

What is sociology?

To the public sociology often appears to be a set of methods, a way of investigating society and its problems. The use of representative surveys, based upon questionnaires or interviews, may seem to be the very trademark of the sociological approach. For those who want to use sociological expertise as a tool in the solution of problems raised in other disciplines (in medicine, economics or law) these methods may appear to be the main contribution of sociology.

From the point of view of sociology this is unsatisfactory. Not that sociologists should be unwilling to provide methodological assistance in collaborative efforts with other scholars or practitioners, but a significant branch of scholarship and research cannot find its identity and *raison d'être* in a package of technical tools. Nor can it be taken for granted that other disciplines, politicians, administrators or the public have most to gain from an emphasis on the methods of sociology.

Leaving aside methods and techniques, one might attempt a definition that refers to the subject matter of sociology. Sociology can be described as the study of society and of social relations. It deals with social issues pertaining to society at large, to nations and even to the world community. And it deals with the interaction that occurs between individuals, or 'actors', as sociologists tend to call the participants in interaction.

This may provide a clue to what sociology is all about, but it does not provide us with sufficient criteria to distinguish sociology from other social sciences. The above description may also fit, more or less accurately, fields such as economics, political science, contemporary history, social psychology or even law. What distinguishes sociology from the other social sciences and makes it in some sense unique is *the special approach* to a subject matter that it shares with other disciplines.

By contrast with the academic disciplines of law, economics or political science, one might claim that the aim of sociology is quite general. Each of the other social sciences is specialized; each of them covers a certain sector or segment of society: the law, the economy, the polity. Sociology is not specialized in this way, although subdivisions have emerged, branches within sociology, that correspond to some extent with these and other sectors. We shall return to the question of the 'hyphenated sociologies', of which the sociology of law is one, alongside such disciplines as medical sociology, family sociology and industrial sociology.

Does the general approach of sociology, encompassing in principle all that goes on in a society, imply that its aim is to develop a synthesis of the other, more specialized social sciences? Some ambition of the kind is discernible in the writings of sociologists, but it is quite clear that sociology cannot compete with the other social sciences with respect to their premises or claim comparable insight into their problems, theories and methods. What separates sociology, more or less clearly, from the other social sciences is not that it encompasses all of social life; it is the way in which it deals with the problems that is its distinguishing mark.

Sociology has developed an approach and corresponding concepts that are not limited in their application to any particular sector of society. From a political, administrative or professional point of view, society presents itself as divided into agencies and institutions, each with its allotted responsibility for handling separate tasks. The members of a society have specialized tasks to perform, and they participate, outside their homes, primarily within one or a few sectors. On the basis of this division of labour, and also as its precondition, a number of scientific disciplines, including the social sciences, have evolved.

Sociology does not belong in any one of these specialized sectors. Its concepts have no special affinity with law, economics, politics, medicine, the military, the family or industry. They are of a general nature. Concepts like action, norm, role, interaction, social system, organization, power, stratification refer to phenomena that occur in the family, in the school, in economic production, distribution and consumption, in the health service, politics, the Army, etc. The goal and the perspective for the future of sociology is to locate and name the elementary bricks of which all social formations are built. Its driving theoretical aim is to erase the fences between sectors of society, to demonstrate the common elements of all social life, or at least to show how they can be expressed through a common vocabulary, a sociological language (one, it is hoped, that will approximate the vernacular).

Earlier we looked at one aspect of sociology's striving in the direction of a general theory of social relations that transcends the sectors and subdivisions of society. This aspect refers in a sense to the internal processes of the various parts of sociology. There is a vague analogy here with nuclear physics, when it turns its attention to the most minute particles of which matter is constituted, but this is a comparison that must not be over-stressed. The other aspect of sociology's drive towards the general consists of attempts to describe and analyse total societies, nations and states, even the world community. This kind of analysis also transcends the borderlines between sectors. The aim is not to present the political system of a country, its religious institutions, its economy, military establishment and so on, but to demonstrate how these sectors are linked together in a larger totality, society itself. Sociology attempts to show how conditions within one sector or one social institution impinge upon, and in turn are influenced by, conditions within other sectors.

Few sociologists, if any, have been able to perform such analyses of whole societies by relying on the fundamental concepts referred to above, concepts that seem most applicable on the micro-sociological level. In their analyses of whole societies and their development scholars usually have (and probably must have) recourse to terms with more colloquial or historical associations. I am thinking of such terms as capitalism, urbanism, secularization, working class, professionalization, etc. It is hardly possible to constitute these terms on the basis of some kind of combination of general micro-sociological concepts. To understand the meaning of these macro-sociological terms (and they may often appear manifold and confusing) one has to be broadly familiar with the society to which they refer.

In our attempt to define the characteristic features of sociology, we have touched upon certain aspects that can cause controversy and friction in its relationships with other professions. In its ambition to describe and analyse total social structures, sociology may appear to lay claim to a certain kind of super-expertise. It may seem to have imperialistic pretentions or at least to be the co-ordinator of the contributions of other social scientists, who may have good reason to question the scientific foundation of such claims. Some will maintain, often justifiably, that in their quest for the general in social life, in their concern with the great perspectives, sociologists remain ignorant of the particular. What do they really know about the economy, the law, the health service or the politics of municipalities? There is undoubtedly a hiatus between the ambitions of sociology and what it can offer in terms of verified findings.

One attempted solution to the dilemma between the concern for the general and for particulars has been the development of the 'hyphenated sociologies'. These subdivisions of sociology have often emerged as appendices to other well established disciplines, the sociology of medicine and of law being two examples of this trend. In other cases sociology has gone in the opposite direction and has created disciplines around topics that were previously unoccupied, so to speak. This is true of family sociology, industrial sociology or community studies, and urban and rural sociology.

The sociology of law, like the other subdivisions of sociology, is marked by tension between the search for the general and the need for specialization as a basis for concrete empirical studies. It ranges from detailed studies of the operation and decision-making of courts or legislative bodies to general theories about the style and function of law as characteristics of whole societies. The sociology of law of necessity reflects the dilemmas and tensions of sociology in general.

In the foregoing it has been tacitly assumed that the sociology of law is a branch of sociology and not of legal studies. This is not a wholly uncontroversial or self-evident point of departure. There are lawyers who look upon the sociology of law as a methodological aid to the solution of legal problems, presumably mainly problems *de lege ferenda,* those of legislators and of commissions that prepare briefs for law-makers. In other words, there exist both a lawyer's sociology of law and a sociologist's sociology of law.

Later in this chapter we shall have occasion to observe the tension between a lawyer's and a sociologist's sociology of law as they appear in divergent conceptual developments in the two fields of scholarship. As for the nature of legal scholarship, certain aspects were discussed at some length in chapter 4. Only a brief comment will be added here as an introduction to some more programmatic statements on the sociology of law.

Legal scholarship

The doctrinal study of law describes positive law in a society at a given time. It orders the valid rules according to a certain system and interprets legal norms with the aid of juridical methods. The legal scholar must also take a stand with respect to certain empirical problems. He will refer to customs and attitudes that are to be found among the members of society. He may also present hypotheses about how legal norms and decisions exert influence on the behaviour and attitudes of people. In addition, he makes statements about what the courts are doing in fact and what they may be expected to do in the future. There is, as has often been pointed out, a normative element in legal scholarship. The legal scholar evaluates various activities and social situations as more or less desirable. He may use traditional and normatively loaded terminology.

In general, it is easy to perceive the practical aims of legal scholarship. Its main function is to enable legal practitioners, counsel (barristers), judges and administrators, to solve concrete legal problems. Evidence of the close bond between legal scholarship and legal practice can also be found in the fact that some of the work done by judges, administrators and barristers is reminiscent of the products of legal scholarship.

A definition of the subject matter of legal scholarship by reference to the positive law of the land and its valid norms may raise certain problems. It is not immediately given which these norms are. Doubts arise concerning the criteria that determine the validity of legal rules. Two lawyers or legal scholars will often hold divergent opinions about whether a norm (derived from customary law or the common law), as expressed in judicial opinion, is or is not valid law. Even more common are debates and differences of opinion as to how statutes are to be interpreted. However, these problems, including the philosophical ones pertaining to the definition of the concept of law, do not prevent lawyers from delimiting a solid nucleus of rules that, beyond much doubt, can be defined as valid law.

The sociology of law

The sociology of law also seeks to describe the positive legal order of a society. However, the sociologist tends to focus his attention upon facts and relationships other than those that are of primary concern to lawyers. The methods he applies when collecting material for his studies are different from the juridical ones, and the goals of his endeavours tend to deviate from those that guide the work of lawyers. None of these differences is absolute, however. Overlaps and combinations do occur.

Traditional legal scholarship, as has been mentioned above, is shaped to a large extent by the needs generated within the practice of law. The relationship of the sociology of law to practical needs and demands is more distant and less clearly patterned. One cannot say that there is a practice of the sociology of law as there is a practice corresponding to legal scholarship. Scholarly work within law may be so practical as to constitute a source of law and to form a basis for the decisions of the courts. Nothing parallel to this can be found within the sociology of law. To arrive at generalizations built on a basis of empirical data is a typical aim of the sociology of law; to reach conclusions that fit a case is not. The method of legal scholarship has a generalizing aspect, while it does at the same time prepare the ground for individualization (for instance, through the analysis of precedents). In the juridical field of discourse one may draw conclusions that point to the solution of concrete problems. A typical result of legal sociological studies is to indicate the possible effects of statutory enactments or of legal decisions that the practitioner, in accordance with his own discretion, must evaluate and combine with other considerations.

Legal scholarship appears to have served its primary function in relation to those who apply and enforce the law. It may seem that the sociology of law is primarily of assistance to those who make law, to those who participate in the legislative process. Those who enforce the law are concerned with individual cases, albeit in accordance with general principles. Those who make laws, whether they be Acts of Parliament or administrative decrees, are concerned with the general consequences, the mass effect, so to speak, of the rules that they make. A similar interest in sociological analysis may also prevail among groups that stand in opposition to the regimes that have the power to legislate and to make decisions about what the law should be. For the sociology of law is not, and should not be, an unthinking handmaid of the powers that be. It has great critical potential.

Legislators are often more concerned with statistical probabilities than with the outcome of individual cases. This points to a link between the methods of the legislator and of the sociologist respectively. One might similarly claim that there is an affinity between the methods of legal scholarship and the intellectual tools of the judge. Once more, however, it should be emphasized that these are differences of degree and not absolute contrasts. For even the professional legislator relies, to a large extent, on the results of legal scholarship.

If the sociology of law is to be regarded as an applied social science, this is likely to be in relation to legislation. Yet the sociology of law is very much concerned with problems that have no close connection with the tasks of practitioners. Actually, its primary goal, in my view, is to cast new light on the general relationship between the law and the society in which it functions. The aim is as much to increase our understanding of how society functions as to improve the techniques available for the solution of practical problems. The sociology of law joins with general sociology in its emphasis on the building up of a store of knowledge and insight into the structure of society, regardless of the immediate tasks to which such knowledge might be put.

Within legal scholarship the impact of legal rules and decisions has often been discussed. Hypotheses about the probable effects of legal enactments abound in connection with the drafting of Bills, the premises of court decisions, administrative documents and the argumentation of legal counsel. The opinions advanced about the different effects of penalties provide examples. Such hypotheses may be advanced as means of finding empirical bases for new legislation, or they may provide teleological grounds for opinions on valid law. The teleological method in jurisprudence implies that the function and impact of a legal norm may become a source of law, alongside precedent and custom. Sometimes such empirical hypotheses can serve as respectable façades for other concerns – the prejudices and interests of lawyers and politicians, for example. Whatever the motives are, the empirical basis of such hypotheses is limited in scope and often of questionable quality.

However, the concern of sociologists of law is relatively independent of the demands of legal practitioners or of those who make law. The basic task of the sociology of law is to investigate invariances in the relationship between legal and other social phenomena.[1] Such investigations need not contribute directly to the solution of legal problems, be they *de lege lata* or *de lege ferenda.* Their main purpose is to increase our understanding of the function of law as a cause of, or hindrance to, social change, as an important ingredient in practically everything that happens in society.

Socio-technique or critical science?

In recent years a debate has raged about the political function of sociology. The discussion has been dominated by arguments for and against what has, for the sake of convenience or for ulterior motives, been termed 'positivism'. Positivism has often been presented, by Marxist and other critics, as a bogey man, a tool of the powers that be, a means of preserving inequality, injustice and structures that subdue individual freedom. By presenting society as it is, founded upon statistical data and other kinds of empirical evidence, it has been maintained that sociology preserves and suppresses where it ought to liberate and initiate change.[2]

Some of this criticism has been shallow and ill-founded, but the debate has brought into focus some real dilemmas, not least for the sociology of law, since law is closely connected with the exercise of power in society. To study law is to study power. And who is to gain by such study — those who exercise power or those who are powerless? From this reasoning it may seem that the sociology of law, in so far as it has political implications, will tend to be a tool in the hands of the government, the legislature and the courts — in short, a means of exerting influence over the premises of the establishment.

Law and legal scholarship are by their very nature, tied to positive law, to the norms and institutions that are established. A legal scholar may contribute some new points of view or shift the interpretation of a statute in a new direction. But these are rather minute amendments to an established state of affairs. As participants in the legislative process, either as politicians or as experts, legal scholars can initiate change, albeit rarely of a radical kind. As scholars, however, they are bound by the law as it exists; it provides the material for their analyses.

The sociology of law is, in this respect, in a different position, offering much more leeway for critical analysis of legal issues. It provides the critic with a stepping-stone, outside the realm of the law itself, an Archimedian point from which he may, if not shake the earth, at least rock the boat. In a programmatic article on the task of the sociology of law published in 1948 I tried to lay down some principles that bear upon the positivist dilemma. The following quotation sprang from a reference to Max Weber's maxim about the value neutrality (*Wertfreiheit*) of social science:

> Irrespective of normative logical premises the work of a scholar may have an impact upon the attitudes of his audience. The influence exerted will tend to have some relevance to values, even if this was not intended. If

nothing else, the research findings may provide people with new tools with which to further causes they believed in before they learned about them.

A critical question is whether the social scientist ought to close his eyes to the possible or probable uses to which his findings may be put, or whether he should try to develop tools suited to the realization of values that are his own. Implicitly a choice between values is made whenever a subject of study is selected. The question is whether we ought to infuse this choice with as much consciousness as possible, or whether it should be made tacitly under the cover of untenable standards of objectivity.

From the moment a scholar opts for doctrinal law as his field of study, he has opted in favour of the established legal system. True enough, there are legal scholars who have advocated legal change, sometimes successfully. But by and large these reformers too have accepted the positively given legal system. Although the quality of the work of these reformers may have been of a high standard, they have rarely been able to support their reformatory endeavours and theories with research findings. When a lawyer enters the area of *de lege ferenda,* he must to a large extent rely upon speculation and common-sense knowledge. . . . This situation proves that there is a need for new methods in legal research. It is an important task to develop a sociology of law capable of satisfying this need. One of its most important functions must be to provide the means by which one may conduct studies *de lege ferenda,* based upon empirical research. Thereby the sociology of law will make it possible to work not only for the established legal system, but also for ideas that modify or contradict it. Such an option is important because it provides a real freedom, corresponding to the formal demand for objectivity.[3]

In chapter 4 it was pointed out that the concept of crime has a status in criminology, including criminal sociology, that differs from the status it has in criminal law. We shall now consider two other concepts that are important to legal scholarship and practice as well as to the sociology of law: property and contracts.

Property

Property is a concept that has played a dominant role throughout a long legal tradition. It has been assigned a focal role by certain schools of sociology, primarily the Marxist. In other schools of sociology the concept of property is not accorded the same priority. As we shall see, other concepts cover some of the same ground.

There are many issues that have important policy implications, in relation to which lawyers and the courts have to take a stand on whether something is a property right or not. For example, do property rights include the traditional right of management in a limited-liability company? Does this right pertain to the shareholders, in the sense that it would be a violation of their property rights if, say, a new set of elected representatives of the employees were to constitute a majority on the board of directors? These questions show that the legal concept of property is still of vital relevance to the settlement of political and administrative problems of considerable urgency. Likewise, the separate concepts of property rights as they appear when divided up into a variety of different types of property, constitute issues that are very much alive. Although the concepts are legal, the sociologist also has to direct his attention to them in the course of his social analyses. What is the relationship between property rights in the legal sense and the concepts that are used by sociologists when they deal with issues of this kind?

The law lumps together under the concept of property such disparate things as the farmer's ownership of land that he tills himself; the home-owners's right to his own house, his car and clothes; the holding of big and small portfolios of stocks in limited-liability companies; cash and bank accounts. All these are classified together, in some relationships anyway, as property rights. On the other hand, the concept of property does not encompass the employee's right to employment. The right of employment (in the sense that as a citizen one can demand work) is not an adjudicable right in Norway, although the Constitution (§ 110) imposes an obligation on the government to secure full employment. The right to a wage is not property but a different kind of obligatory right.

The tenant's right to continued lease of his home is protected by statutory provisions but is not considered a property right. However, because of a great and growing emphasis on apartments as objects of investment an array of new legal arrangements is developing, from property rights in the traditional sense to various kinds of lease that have property-like overtones. These changes take the shape of contractual inventions.

Property does not seem to include the Australian aborigine's right to the clan domain[4] or the Lapp's right to pasture fields, according to the prevailing view of the courts; nor does property right include the right of professional monopoly. The latter poses the problem of the kind of right one has in one's own education.

One aspect of the right is to make it exclusive by a procedure of certification as a condition to perform in a profession. But this is a collective right and is not considered a property right in the legal sense.

This brief sketch shows that property in the legal sense encompasses phenomena that are very different, ranging from the big shareholder's right to steer his company, employ people and decide how to use the plant, to rights in one's own clothes and in household utensils. These are, legally speaking, the same kind of right. On the other hand, the concept of property excludes many kinds of access to resources that are of vital importance to people but are construed under other labels.

From the sociologist's point of view, what are the concepts and terms that are to be used when we speak about these problems? 'Access to resources' was the term I used. It is not a technically defined sociological concept but rather a term borrowed from the media and from political debate. However, sociologists increasingly use it when they deal with the macro-sociological problems of distribution, equality and class. Instead of access to resources, one could speak of 'level of welfare', and one could use other terms, like 'wealth', to refer to the same phenomena. But whatever terms are used by sociologists, they are used in a way that does not correspond to the legal concept of property.

Wealth or access to material resources is only one aspect of the sociological problem associated with property. Another aspect that sociologists deal with in this context is leadership, command or management of organizations, especially organizations of production. Here, as Marx emphasized, and after him Renner, the question of power arises.[5]

A third problem concerns the relationship between property and identity. Property rights have been linked with social identity, and identity is a vital sociological issue. As a sociological issue, however, it is dealt with in a more general sense. Identity can be linked with property (for example, one's home and garden), but is perhaps more often, and more strongly, linked with work. Furthermore, identity can be linked with ethnic or class origin, and it can be defined in various other ways as a social extension of the means by which the self is supported.[6]

Property and the right to work

Let us take as our starting-point the questions of how people obtain access to resources, and what the implications are for the equality or inequality of their distribution. What are the vital legal concerns of people in their everyday lives? One can observe a significant historical shift from conditions in which the relationship with property was pivotal. This was true in agrarian society, not long gone. Property rights in land were extremely important, and for those who did not own land, the private contracts they had with the property owners were of decisive importance. The tenant's, the crofter's, the sharecropper's or agricultural worker's contracts with the landowner were the focal legal arrangements that determined the individual's welfare. The individual's – or the family's – access to resources was dependent either directly upon property rights or upon individual contracts with a proprietor. To a large extent this was also the case with craftsmen and merchants in the towns. It was through property rights or through private arrangements with property owners that people gained and maintained access to resources.

The situation has changed a great deal. Recent studies of living conditions indicate that what determines access to resources and standards of living is access to work, the number of hours of work per year and the kind of work that is being performed.[7] Access to employment has become the primary avenue to resources. Work still often depends upon contracts with property owners, of course, so the question of property has not been rendered unimportant. I shall return to the changes that have taken place in contractual arrangements.

The comparison of property with work raises the question of the status of work as an inalienable human right. Is that description in tune with the needs of people today and with the mechanisms that lead to a certain distribution of resources in society? The right to work is in many respects protected – for example, through the prohibition of the discharge of employees on unacceptable grounds. But 'reasonable cause' for discharge can be a rather elastic concept. If employees find some of their work mates unacceptable (for example, because they are political extremists with an unpleasant missionary zeal), the threat of a strike may provide the management with an economically motivated cause for discharge. There is now weaker protection of the right to work than of the right to property.

Protection against discharge is one question. Another is the question of the right to employment of those who are not employed, who are outside the labour market but want to enter it. As I have already mentioned, in Norway there is no enforceable and inalienable right to demand work in spite of a symbolic clause (§110) in the Constitution. If such a right were to develop, how should it be elaborated with respect to distance from one's home and as regards one's qualifications? These are very difficult problems from the point of view of the law. The technical requirements of the rule of law render it difficult to make the right to work justiciable in the sense that it could be presented as an individual human right in a court of law. There are, of course, other obstacles in the way of establishing access to work as a human right, since it could easily conflict with strong economic interests. And the responsibility of the government would be a heavy burden for any political leadership.

All this notwithstanding, access to work is today a more vital need for people than most of the property rights that are so well protected. There is little correspondence between the rights that have been regarded historically as rights that deserve strong, constitutional protection and those rights which have developed later but today are more important. True, property rights are being eroded, and there is a growing tendency to consider some of them as no longer worthy of protection; equally there is increasing awareness of the need to protect more effectively some of the other types of access to resources.

One of the reasons why it is difficult to protect the right to work is that protection would, almost by necessity, entail a duty to work. Work may seem desirable when you are unemployed, but when you are working it often appears to be a burden rather than a privilege. About work there is an ambivalence that is not associated with property. Property is more unequivocally a value, since one can buy anything with money. Therefore property may seem more worthy of protection even to those who would objectively speaking, have more to gain from secure access to work.

Legal techniques, legislative as well as adjudicative, are well suited to handling problems associated with money or problems that can be converted in money values. The law can, for example, deal fairly effectively with compensation in cases of unemployment. To provide work itself can hardly be guaranteed in a society in which market forces play a dominant role. To work is to be placed within a comprehensive network of economic and social relationships. To arrange this network of relationships so as to assure everybody such a place seems to be beyond the capacity of existing legislative, administrative and adjudicative techniques in capitalist and mixed-economy societies.

There is still another problem. The right to work would necessitate the institution of *new* rights. There is something legally self-evident about the traditional rights. They are historically given; they may be non-sensical, illogical or in violation of many human interests, but they are *there.* Those who want to develop new conceptualizations, those who want to change the law or to modify legal theory in order to make plans for legal change carry the onus. They have to prove that their proposals are superior to the tradition and worth the costs involved in the change.

We may say that it is unjust that some people should inherit shares. Shareholders do not, as a rule, make much profit today, but they have a share in the management of the firm, which seems irrational. But does a better system exist? As a matter of fact, it is no easy task to conceive of a better system, and it might be even harder to convince the majority of the population that any one of various alternative systems is to be preferred. And against the dilemmas and conflicts of interest that are awakened by such situations of choice stands *Die normative Kraft des Faktischen* as a relief from uncertainty and responsibility.

In law generally there are many instances in which the passage of time acquires a normative character – as in the establishment of old usage as customary law, deadlines for making valid claims, the obsolescence of rights and obligations, the acquiring title of through usage and *desuetudo.* The historical character of the basic legal concepts embedded in Constitutions and Bills of Rights testifies to the force inherent in the passing of time. I think it is one of the tasks of sociology to challenge this tradition and to regroup associated phenomena in terms of their relationship to vital human interests. In the long run this sociological rationality may have an impact on legal conceptualizations.

Property and political rights

Property is one type of access to resources. Other avenues to resources, with a more or less distant relationship with property, are becoming more prevalent for the majority of the people. One might even say that citizenship as such has become the most basic avenue to resources in the so-called welfare states. If people don't get work, they do get money and are assured of a standard of living that at least prevents them from starving. The right to citizenship is fundamental, both in the sense that citizenship ensures a minimum of social security and in the sense that decisions concerning access to work and wage levels are increasingly being made either by public authorities or through collective bargaining between big organizations. This means that participatory political rights are more and more taking the place of individual rights of property or contract.

Although each employee has an individual contract, the fate of that contract, its content and significance, is determined through collective bargaining and decisions made by the government. Access to resources becomes very much a question of how much say a citizen has in collective bargaining or in the decisions of public authorities. The Canadian political scientist MacPherson has claimed that political rights should now be seen as property because they are taking the place of property.[8] One could say of shareholder's rights that they have always been political rights, although of a different kind from the franchise, since some property owners have much more of a say than others. The principle of one-man-one-vote does not apply. But even big shareholders have to persuade a majority on the board to accept their preferred policies, as they are unable to make decisions about the firm simply on the basis of their shares.

Property as right of management

This leads us to the question of property as a foundation for authority. One of Marx's great achievements was that he saw clearly that ownership of the means of production entailed the right to command a workforce. In legal theory this viewpoint has been elaborated upon by Karl Renner in a very interesting way.[9]

Property rights, which seem to be rights in some kind of material property, turn out in fact to be a right to semi-military command. Today military command may not be the most correct analogy, but property is still one of the bases of authority.

Sociologists tend to classify property as one among several sources of authority. Power, authority and management are the unifying concepts. Within a theory of power, management and organization, several issues arise. Does it make any difference to the exertion of power whether one owns property as a shareholder or as a sole owner, or whether one is employed by the government to manage a firm as in socialist countries? Do such differences fundamentally change the authority relationship? Does the worker have more of a say in socialist than in capitalist countries? Do the experts play a similar role under both kinds of system, irrespective of whether the experts are owners, are employed by owners or are employed by the government?

Sociologists have developed general theories of organizations that are more interesting than theories about the ownership of the means of production. Firms and factories are dealt with as a sub-type of a more general type of organization, in which one can also include government departments, universities, hospitals and prisons. Some structural patterns and processes may be common to most organizations; others will differ, and one can ask to what extent the differences are related to property and to specific property forms and to what extent other aspects of the organizations explain the differences.

Here again we see that there is a discrepancy between the way in which sociologists tend to group phenomena and the way in which law has grouped them. Political discussion has to a large extent been steered into certain channels by traditional legal definitions of the problems. It makes a great difference whether the structure of the private firm is discussed as a problem of property rights and their limitations or as a problem of power and its legitimacy. People often feel powerless; they are weary of the very concept of power and sceptical towards people in power. Property rights, on the other hand, are considered vital, if not as an avenue to access to resources, then as a basis of consumption. Today there is much more property to go around than there ever has been before. And there are more property owners, if we consider as property rights the means of consumption (houses, cars, etc.). As a general concept, property may enjoy more unanimous support in the welfare states today than it ever has. Thus the rivalry between traditional law and sociology over the choice of basic concepts may be more than an academic exercise.

Property and identity

I shall not say much about the question of property and identity. Sociologists deal with identity as a general problem with ramifications that relate to property, work, sex or the more intangible question of ethnic identity and the right to be the kind of person one thinks one is on the basis of genealogy or class membership.

Within this wider framework there are specific problems that arise in connection with property as a basis of identity — for example, its alienability as compared with sex and genealogy. In contrast to other bases of identity, such as work, the property of the rich can be spread both geographically and functionally and can thus provide opportunities for them to 'participate' simultaneously, and vicariously, in many different activities. This aspect of property, ignored by law and economics, becomes salient in terms of sociological types of conceptualization.

Contracts

The relationship between the legal concept of a contract and the kindred sociological concepts of exchange and reciprocity is a vast topic. Here I shall attend only to a few problems that are parallel to, and partly derived from, those arising out of property rights. When property rights establish relationships of authority and domination, they do so through the agency of contracts. In exchange for a wage employees contractually bind themselves to accept the right of management of the legal owner of the means of production. It was suggested above that legal conceptions of property have not taken sufficient cognizance of this aspect of certain types of ownership. It may be claimed that modern labour law builds to a larger extent on an understanding of the social realities of the relationship between management and workers and, more generally, between employers and employees.

The liberal legal conception of a contract was formerly that it was an agreement entered into freely by two parties on the basis of presumed equality. During the last hundred years there has been a growing recognition on the part of legislators that labour contracts are not entered into on the basis of the real equality of both parties and real freedom of choice. Thus we have witnessed a new trend in legal development, starting with the protection of children in industry.

Legislation has followed the social trend towards more equality between organized labour and organized management. In collective bargaining the presumption of equality, albeit very hard to gauge with any precision, does not seem to be drastically misleading. However, the applicability of old contractual models becomes much more dubious when we look at the relationship between the worker and the manager or owner from the point of view of the individual wage earner, to whom the main agreement between his trade union and the employers' association presents itself very much like a statutory enactment. Its clauses are not negotiable; he must take them or leave them. His say in the matter is limited to his participatory rights in his shop and his union, among them the right to participate in voting over proposed agreements on wages and other conditions of work. Likewise, when he is on the job he is faced with a blueprint for the running of the firm and a number of routines that are not negotiable. He has to accept, more or less wholesale, the totality of his situation as a wage earner, which is subservient to the system of authority and the division of labour.

It seems inappropriate, from a sociological point of view, to deal with the situation as one of contractual consent. If we claim that the way in which labour relations actually develop within a firm or, for that matter, within a public facility depends upon the consent of the contracting parties, this does not yield a proper sociological framework for analysis. 'Consent' then assumes a very artificial meaning. The problem and its clarification would be better served if we looked upon collective agreements and the plans for work as authoritative rules, much like statutes. The real questions are whether participatory rights are effective, and to what extent the organizational structures of trade unions and firms permit the intentions of employers and employees to manifest themselves in relationships of reciprocity. For just as the worker finds that most of his concrete rights and obligations at work are non-negotiable, so the employer finds that he has to accept traits and activities among the workforce that he did not think that he had bargained for.

From the point of view of sociology, we are faced once more with problems pertaining to membership of organizations rather than to dyadic relationships of exchange. The contractual paraphernalia hide not only the realities of authority but also the realities of how authority may be circumvented. The literature on informal organization in the firm, the establishment of production ceilings and other social norms, cannot be interpreted in terms other than those of organizational theory and the analysis of systems.[10] In legal terms it remains a question limited to the scope and content of the contractual instruments that guide the relationship.

In recent years the problems of inequality in contractual relationships have expanded beyond the sphere of production to include that of consumption or consumer protection. To an increasing degree, the buyer of a product is faced with a standard contract formulated by a large company, or even by an association of producers (for example, insurance companies or airlines). The small print on the back of contracts has become a legendary trap. Since competition, at least from the point of view of the individual consumer, is often limited or even absent altogether, the terms of these standardized contracts resemble those of legislative enactments. The consumer has to accept them and, as is the case with respect to many statutes, frequently without knowing or understanding what he has accepted, especially if something goes wrong.

The first attempts to deal with this kind of a situation on the part of the courts, were based loosely on assumption that the buyer has not consented freely to the terms of such contracts. In Scandinavian law, a general clause has traditionally rendered immoral contracts (contracts that contravene the canons of decency) invalid. Contracts concerning games of chance and bets have long been unenforceable according to Norwegian law (with the recent exception of the national lotteries and the pools). Today there are general clauses in Scandinavian contract law that render unreasonable contracts unenforceable.

This latter type of clause represents a departure from the liberal conception of a contract, since it interferes directly with the content of the exchange, unlike most of the traditional norms, which merely laid down rules about the process in and between the parties effecting a contract. It is characteristic that the aim of abolishing unfair contracts is also sought and achieved through statutory prohibitions accompanied by penal sanctions. Those who charge an 'unreasonable' price for their commodity or service are liable to penalty.

The rules that protect the free will of consenting parties aim at the maintenance of a market in which self-interest is the driving force and competition the mechanism through which self-interest is translated into the common good. Rules that seek to do away with unfair contracts must, in so far as they are motivated by a desire to redress the balance between unequal contracting parties, be viewed in a different perspective. Their purpose is to further equality generally through the reduction of existing inequalities, for free contracts tend to perpetuate, or even augment, the prevailing differences by a process of cumulation: 'To those who have shall be given', 'The poor pay more.'[11]

From this point of view, standard contracts present themselves as legal instruments that contribute systematically and statistically to the determination of the distribution of welfare in society. They are part of the more general mechanisms of social stratification that further equality or inequality between citizens. To deal with them in terms of dyadic exchange is less interesting than to view them as parts of these larger macro-sociological processes.

Labour contracts establish social relationships and systems of a certain duration. Thus it is fairly clear that legal problems over contracts can and should be translated into sociological problems of organization and hierarchical authority. Sales contracts, on the other hand, often establish no more than the most ephemeral of relationships. They do not, normally, add up to the establishment of social systems. If competition prevails, which may often be in doubt, the relationship between seller and customer is, as a matter of principle, highly vulnerable in a free market, where a sales contract is an instrument that permits exchange to take place as an isolated event with no past and no future. Lack of loyalty is an in-built characteristic of the relationship, yet it is part of the stuff of which social solidarity is constituted, as is made quite explicit by Durkheim's term 'organic solidarity'.[12]

Moreover, in law it is recognized that contracts are not all cut from the same cloth. From the marriage contract, via the labour contract, to the standardized sales contract legal constructions undergo considerable change. But we were on the verge of discerning an even more drastic contradiction between the sociological implications of labour and sales contracts respectively. Labour contracts establish social systems, while sales contracts are based upon premises that deny lasting ties. However, on closer inspection the difference, albeit highly significant, must be couched in other terms.

Labour contracts and, even more, marriage contracts establish systems of interacting individuals. Depending upon the type of industry, its location and the situation in the labour market, the duration of employment may vary considerably. But the ideals governing personnel policy emphasize, on the whole, the advantages of lasting bonds between employer and employee. A high turnover of staff is considered a cost, a disadvantage. Sales contracts also build systems, but not in the same sense. They contribute to the emergence and maintenance of highly standardized roles, the incumbents of which may differ very considerably. Standard contracts and the fairly universal price and quality of goods in many retail outlets indicate the extent to which competition, the opportunity to shop around, has led to the uniform performance of sales organizations. Paradoxically, it is precisely the mechanisms of a free market that militate against the development of personal loyalties and further both the equalization of expectations and the response to equalization through the mechanisms of supply and demand.

The ephemeral nature of relationships built upon sales contracts leads to the establishment of very stable expectations at the level of norms and roles. A counter-example would be the engagement or betrothal agreement, which is unenforceable in modern Scandinavian family law. It is not recognized as a contract in spite of the relatively profound and durable relationship that it often symbolizes. An assumption of loyalty is built into the reciprocal understandings of the couple. Engagement also represents a withdrawal from the free marriage market, an end to shopping around, an end to competition. The limitations on the freedom of the erotic market must, in part, account for the idiosyncratic, unpredictable and unstable nature of mutual expectations and responses to such expectations.

The upshot of this brief excursion into the field of contracts is that there are very profound sociological distinctions between what are, legally speaking, only different kinds of the same species. Furthermore, we should note that there is no natural sociological counterpart to the field covered by the legal concept of contract.

Systems in legal and sociological thought

Some two centuries ago legal theory, which was at the time permeated by notions of natural law, branched off in two new directions. On the foundations of natural law Adam Smith established a new science of economics and an ideology of the free market.[13] A little later Jeremy Bentham, while declaring his opposition to the natural law of Blackstone, created a new science of legislation based upon the calculus of utilities, which was in practice closely related to the calculus of utilities which underpinned economic thinking.[14]

In retrospect, Adam Smith appears to have been the founding father of modern economics, a branch of learning of which the pattern of growth and development has been similar, at least superficially, to that of a natural science. Economics has turned out to be a cumulative science, showing a pronounced capacity to preserve, systematize and learn from past experiences. It is also cumulative in the sense that it has provided a basis for large organizations occupied with the gathering and analysis of masses of economic data in a more or less concerted, albeit not too successful, effort to predict and control.

In his time Bentham seemed, as much as Adam Smith, to be in the process of laying the foundations of a new social science of legislation. In retrospect, however, his appears to have been a lone voice in the wilderness as he advocated the sociological study of the impact of legislation, although his general approach had great influence upon the legislators of his time.

The social science of legislation has not advanced much since the time of Bentham, although the number of trained lawyers has increased enormously. Laws have been systematized to a high degree, and the internal logic of the legal system has been made more consistent. New Bills are carefully drafted with the assistance of legal experts as well as of a variety of fact-finding agencies and personnel. But these efforts lack the cumulative impact that can be perceived in the growth of economics. If there is a cumulative tendency, it is embodied in statutory law itself rather than in legal, let alone socio-legal, scholarship.

Deterrence is one of the topics on which Bentham shed considerable light. In recent years studies have been conducted that, as isolated pieces of research, are unarguably superior to Bentham's speculations. In these studies the researchers have employed formidable statistical techniques and sophisticated methods of data-gathering. But the general theory of deterrence has not progressed much, if at all, since Bentham. There is little advice to be gained from research on where, or how, or with what kinds of sanction one might influence people to comply with the law.[15] And there is even less illumination to be gained on theoretical issues that arise in this area.

Why has this situation arisen, and why is it so different from the picture we have of economics as a science? The issue cannot be explained simply in terms of the failure of lawyers who are rooted in the conservatism of the profession to utilize a scientific approach. It must have something to do with the essential differences between the subject matter of the sciences: the market and the law.

The market is a system in a sense in which law is not a system. Changes in certain parts of the market system have calculable repercussions on other parts of the system. All values can be translated into money. By contrast, the law is a system in a vague, logical or quasi-logical sense. It is the task of legal personnel, including legislators, to uphold and develop this systematic aspect of the law. Some have presented it as a deductive system. But that is claiming too much. Whatever one may say about the degree of consistency in the law, it is a system of words, terms, concepts and rules; it is not a system of action or behaviour. Legal scholarship may deal with the system in the normative sense, but the sociology of law does not. That is one reason for the apparent lack of theoretical structure within the sociological study of the law.

The latter point may be illustrated by the fact that a legal system is consistent or inconsistent irrespective of whether non-compliant acts are frequent or not, at least within certain wide limits. Traditional legal scholarship does not deal in terms of frequencies. Whether a type of case occurs once in a decade or many times a day does not matter from the point of view of the lawyer. In the market frequencies are vital: every transaction counts as a contribution to the GNP.

When we concern ourselves with the social impact of legislation, we have to deal with frequencies. How many motorists drive in an intoxicated state under specified conditions with respect to rules, inspections and sanctions? If such a question can be answered, the answer remains an isolated finding without known (or even knowable) repercussions. The fact that the law with respect to drunken driving is logically consistent with the other parts of the criminal law is little help. However, one can dimly perceive that if an increased level of non-compliance with the law requires more supervising personnel on the roads or more space in the prisons, this would, in a way that is reminiscent of the market, have consequences for the opportunity to pursue other legal aims. Controls and sanctions are scarce resources, and there may be regularities in their distribution. They may be translated into taxpayers' money.

One difficulty with an economic approach to the social impact of legislation is that some sanctions, like the death penalty, are cheap in terms of money but very costly in human and political terms. An even more serious difficulty is that there is no common denominator on the effect side. How could one make a comparison between a reduction in drunken driving, resulting in a lower accident rate, and a reduction in shoplifting or tax evasion, let alone the non-payment of debts. The market necessarily involves quantification, whereas the law does not. The two disciplines speak different languages. The sociologist has barely embarked on the task of translating the various values involved in law-making, law enforcement and legal impact, and we do not know what his chances of success are.

To sum up, the market and the law have been presented as two different kinds of system, while it was claimed that the sociology of law cannot be seen as a study of a system, either of the normative or of the behavioural kind. The sociological concept of a system might be of either kind. On the basis of the concepts of norms and roles, one might construe a kind of cultural system akin to the legal system but encompassing a much wider range of normative phenomena. On the basis of the concept of action, it is possible to construe a behavioural system but one that would have much wider scope than the market.

The reason why the market may, with some justification, be seen as a system is the presence of a common denominator of value – money. The reason why the law may, also with some justification, be seen as a normative system is that it is continually the object of a vast, fairly concerted effort to erase or ameliorate inconsistencies. The systemic character of the market, as well as of the law, is a matter of degree. There can be no doubt, for example, that the legal system is a far cry from an axiomatic mathematical or logical system.

Whether we look upon society, the nation, in cultural or interactionist terms, the conditions favouring the application of a systemic approach are much weaker than in the case of the market and the law. No common denominator of values exists, and the culture of a society is not under the care of any one authority or profession. Nevertheless, within sociology the drive is to develop concepts and analytical tools that permit more systemic analysis. However, such analyses can only be carried out if society as such is the object of the study. It is hard to see how one could find social systems within the framework of the hyphenated sociologies. With respect to the sociology of law, some reasons for this conclusion have been given above.

Notes

1 I agree with Lon Fuller, however, when he points out that one aim of the sociology of law is to analyse the law itself as a sociological phenomenon. Chapters 3 and 4 illustrate this. See Lon L. Fuller, 'Some unexplored social dimensions of the law', presented as a contribution to a symposium on Law and the Social Sciences held on 22 September 1967 in connection with the Sesquicentennial Celebration of the Harvard Law School. Cf. also Lawrence M. Friedman, and Stuart Macauly, *Law and the Behavioral Sciences,* 2nd edn. (New York: Bobbs-Merrill, 1977), pp. 829–977.

2 A point of view forcefully represented in the so-called Frankfurt School. Cf. Jürgen Habermas, 'Kritische und konservative Aufgaben der Soziologie', in *Theorie und Praxis. Sozialphilosophische Studien* (Neuwied am Rhein/Berlin: Luchterhand, 1967), pp. 215–30.

3 Vilhelm Aubert, 'Noen problemområder i rettssosiologien' (Problem Areas of the Sociology of Law), *Tidsskrift for rettsvitenskap,* 61 (1948), pp. 435–6.

4 *Milirrpum* v. *Nabalco Pty. Ltd and the Commonwealth of Australia* (Gove land rights case): a claim by aborigines that their interests in certain land had been invaded unlawfully by the defendants. Judgment of the Honourable Mr Justice Blackburn. Supreme Court of Northern Territory, *Federal Law Reports,* 1971.

5 Karl Renner, *The Institutions of Private Law and their Social Functions,* ed. O. Kahn-Freund (London: Routledge & Kegan Paul, 1949), pp. 105ff.

6 Vilhelm Aubert, *Elements of Sociology* (London: Heinemann, 1970), pp. 57–60.
7 *Levekårsundersøkelsen* (The Study of Standard of Living in Norway) (Oslo/Bergen/Tromsø: Universitetsforlaget, 1976), esp. p. 27.
8 C. B. MacPherson, 'Capitalism and the changing concept of property', in Eugene Kamenka, and R. S. Neale (eds.), *Feudalism, Capitalism and Beyond* (Canberra: Australian National University Press), 1975, pp. 104–24.
9 Renner, *The Institutions of Private Law,* pp. 105ff.
10 Philip Selznick, with the collaboration of Philippe Nonet and Howard M. Vollmer, *Law, Society and Industrial Justice* (New York: Russell Sage Foundation, 1969).
11 David Caplowitz, *The Poor Pay More* (New York: Free Press, 1967).
12 Emile Durkheim, *The Division of Labor in Society* (Glencoe, Ill.: Free Press, 1964).
13 Adam Smith, *An Inquiry into the Nature and Causes of the Wealth of Nations* (London: 1776).
14 Jeremy Bentham, *A Fragment on Government and an Introduction to the Principles of Morals and Legislation,* ed. Wilfred Harrison (Oxford: Basil Blackwell, 1948).
15 Cf. Johs. Andenæs, 'General prevention revisited'. *Journal of Criminal Law and Criminology,* 66 (1975), pp. 338–65.

CHAPTER 6

The legal approach – an evaluation

In the preceding chapters I have attempted to outline the characteristics of the legal approach without, strictly speaking, trying to evaluate it in terms of its social usefulness or other criteria. In chapters 1 and 2 law was interpreted as a response to very general – nay, universal – human needs, but very little could be said about the adequacy of the response, since the concern was with law in an abstract sense. Towards the end of chapter 2 there emerged a pattern in the legal structures that is associated with the rule of law, a pattern that seems to have arisen out of the dominant social forces during the period of the *Rechtsstaat* (the law state). Chapters 3 and 4 dealt with more technical problems: the relationship between the demands for conflict-solving institutions and the structure of legal thinking. In chapter 5 this discussion was pursued through a review of the relationship between the legal and the sociological approach.

Implicit in the analysis in this book there are, no doubt, many evaluative elements, appreciative or critical of the legal approach. In this chapter I shall be more explicit about the questions of utility and value. There are two ways of going about this task, the empirical and the normative. An empirical evaluation would base its conclusions upon a study of three questions: to what extent, and how, a society relies upon juridical instruments and institutions, and to what extent its citizens seek recourse to the law when they have grievances to air. A normative evaluation might, of course, lead to different conclusions from those that would perhaps follow from the empirical functionalist approach.

Now, it is a truism that normative or evaluative deductions cannot be made from purely empirical premises. Nevertheless, the priority given to legal institutions by the political leadership of a society, as well as by its individual members, throws light upon questions of value, even if such information does not settle the issues.

The changing role of law and lawyers in the nineteenth and twentieth centuries

I shall start by presenting some material on the changing role of law and lawyers in Norway during a period from the beginning of the last century and up to our own time.

It would not be very misleading to maintain that nineteenth-century Norwegian society was led by lawyers. They were dominant in the Cabinet and the Civil Service, and they were also well represented in Parliament. Industry and commerce were relatively weakly developed, but as development got started lawyers played an active role also in business.

In 1815 there were 329 university-trained lawyers in Norway.[1] At that time there were approximately 400 ministers, 700 military officers, 160 medical doctors and 100 high-school teachers. In terms of numbers, the lawyers were still lagging behind the two older groups of experts — the clergy and the military officers. But they were on the verge of taking over hegemony at the University, in the academic world generally, in the Civil Service and in Norwegian politics. In the period 1815–29 more lawyers than theologians left university with a degree. During the following decades there was a continuous increase, so that the graduates in law numbered more than the graduates from all other faculties combined. On the whole, this was the situation up to as late as the turn of the century. If one might claim that the University of Copenhagen was a school of priests in the eighteenth century, it might be claimed that the University of Oslo until this century had as its foremost educational task the training of lawyers. This is often overlooked in the history of the University, perhaps because there have always been very few teachers in relation to the number of students in the faculty of law.

Such a quantitative description might lead to an overemphasis upon the importance of law around the dawn of industrialism in Norway. It seems likely that the number of lawyers increased not so much in response to a specific demand for legal skills and services but rather as a reaction to a general and rather diffuse need for people with some kind of higher education. The training of lawyers in Norway, as well as in some Continental countries, has probably served functions similar to those that have been served by the public-school system in Britain.[2] Legal education implied, above all, general training in the running of a society, and it has served to establish and consolidate a social network in the higher social strata. In a certain limited sense, these social networks may have served a nationally integrating function.

If we wish to explain why lawyers were the first large group of academically trained experts to expand at the time of the industrial breakthrough, it is necessary to emphasize that it was cheap to train lawyers – much cheaper than to train engineers, natural scientists, doctors or even humanists. Three or four professors sufficed to train all the Norwegian lawyers, and they had little need of facilities. They needed no laboratories, only a few books. Add to this the fact that law, as it has been taught in Scandinavia, has a rather general educational aim, which may meet the demands in a society in the first stages of the process of industrialization and urbanization. In this phase of economic development specialization is poorly developed, and it is difficult to predict and satisfy the need for highly specialized experts. There is a need for jacks-of-all-trades at a high level.

Here it must be pointed out that to be a graduate of law and to be a legal specialist are not exactly the same thing. A hundred years ago, and for that matter even today, people with degrees in law are employed in a wide variety of occupations. And a legal training is often not directly relevant to the field in which the lawyer later will function. Nevertheless, it can be maintained that the legal model of society and legal methods of conflict resolution played a very significant role in nineteenth-century Norwegian society.

In the present debate about the developing countries many regret the large number of philosophers and humanists in India or the abundance of lawyers in many African states while the recruitment of engineers and agronomists lags behind. Precisely from this modern perspective it is interesting to note that the expansion of the legal profession, in terms of numbers and importance, set in before what can properly be termed the 'industrial revolution'. Although in 1814, when the Union with Denmark was severed, Norway was an old state and not to be compared directly with the new African states, very intensive nation-building took place throughout the last century. This integration of Norwegian society in the last century was a decisive precondition for the economic growth that we have enjoyed during this century. Means of communication, schools, a developed Civil Service and judiciary, a system of public health, institutions of credit are well-known preconditions for economic growth. Behind all these factors, however, we find a more general social phenomenon, which is of great significance in many contexts: *trust.*[3]

In a rural society the people will trust their kin, their neighbours and a few figures of authority. However, there are few social bonds capable of creating a basis for trust beyond this limited circle. From this derives a large number of difficulties when new economic enterprises are to be established. Credit, commerce, the loyal payment of taxes, contracts of work, the establishment of banks and limited liability companies presuppose that it is possible to establish trust between people who have not been able to test each other's reliability through personal contact over a period of years. The preconditions for the growth of trust, which can make the nation into a common market, are many. However, I venture to propose the hypothesis that the growth of a fairly large legal profession in Norway contributed to establish this trust at certain points in the social structure where this was a critical precondition. This took place in part as a consequence of the participation of lawyers in the establishment and development of the governmental apparatus itself, including the judiciary. Implicit in this development and in the increasing use of legal methods, lay an emphasis on the increased predictability in social life that is one of the conditions of trust. It also seems likely that the distribution of lawyers in a variety of sectors of social life (for example, private business as well as in government) contributed to the reduction of sources of conflict that otherwise might have had a disintegrating effect.

I speak here about integration within one social class, not across the boundaries of social classes. It was especially in the leading strata of society that lawyers contributed to integration, mutual understanding, increased trust and confidence. Between the classes lawyers have probably not contributed much to mutual understanding — often quite the opposite.

In spite of the strictly class-bound attitudes of lawyers and their participation in the class antagonisms, the nationally integrating function of lawyers may still have been important. The lower social classes at this period constituted no serious political force. They had too little organizational strength and power to make it politically necessary to develop a machinery of conflict resolution to deal with class conflicts. This problem became acute only at a later time. By and large the solution was sought in terms of political means, although also in legal institutions like the Labour Court.

We shall observe some later trends of development later, but first I shall mention some trends that indicate that law has assumed increasing importance. In the period from 1814 to 1960 the number of lawyers increased by a factor of 17, while the population increased by a factor of 4. A Civil Service recruited by lawyers has expanded greatly. Likewise, the scope of legislation has increased a great deal. In the post-war period four to five times as many Bills have passed through Parliament each year as compared with the situation a hundred years ago. One might also point to the spread of legal or quasi-legal procedures in many private organizations, some of which resemble the procedures applied by the courts.

These are significant trends. However, I would tend to emphasize some tendencies that indicate that law has lost in significance, with respect particularly to a decline in the application of legal methods in the more strictly professional sense. This trend started a long time ago in certain areas, while it has become apparent only quite recently in others.

In 1814 there were about a hundred judges in Norway. One hundred and fifty years later this number had only doubled. If we view the judge as an expert who has a service to offer (namely, the peaceful solution of conflicts), it is striking that there has been so little growth in the judiciary, even if we take into consideration the fact that the efficiency of the courts has increased and that they have been relieved of many administrative tasks. This stands in marked contrast to the tendencies in other professional fields, where there has been a great increase in the supply of services. Such is the situation in medicine, in engineering, in architecture, in various branches of the teaching profession and with respect to economic advice of various kinds. Such too was the situation with respect to the services of advocates until quite recently.

However, to emphasize the service aspect of the courts is one-sided. Simultaneously they exert power. In many situations the courts appear to be the defenders of the rights of the little man, while in others they seem to be threatening figures of authority, which mete out penalties or release other kinds of unpleasant sanction, ultimately supported by the threat of naked force. It is therefore not clear whether a welfare state is one that has a large court system or a small one.

This ambiguity is not caused simply by the fearful consequences of some of the verdicts of the courts. It is also related to the fact that the solution of conflicts is not primarily a service offered to any particular individual. Every case has two sides, and legal decisions are characterized by the fact that what is gained by one side must appear as a loss to the other. While medical, technical and pedagogical innovations may lead to the long-term expansion of one or other aspect of human welfare, even the most refined legal techniques do not guarantee increased utility for any particular individual. The service that society is rendered when first-class legal methods are being applied (for example, by the judge) is of a less tangible kind, and society as such is the beneficiary. The most important service is the consolidation of the rule of law.

Although it seems that a modern society must have at least as great a need for highly developed methods of conflict resolution as a pre-industrial society, it is difficult to localize this need. Very serious problems of measurement are raised by attempts to evaluate the effects and functions of a legal system. This may also be one of the reasons why in Norway it is possible to make such extensive use of the judge assistant, who normally comes to the bench fresh from his graduation and without much practical experience. After a few months of service he may take over a very substantial number of cases from the judge, and not the most trivial and simple types of case.

When the institution of the judge assistant was introduced more than a century ago, the intention was that he should be an apprentice and a secretary for the judge, not his equal. However, the growth both of the population and of cases has exerted pressure on the judge to delegate more independent authority to him. The system has functioned well in the sense that few serious criticisms have been levelled at the institution in spite of the fact that in

Norwegian society it is most unusual to delegate so much authority to very young people. Although there may be reason to believe that the apprentice is about as well qualified as the older judge, it is surprising that more serious demands for reform have not been raised. This may be related to the belief that it is impossible to increase the beneficial effects of the courts through improvements in the formal qualifications of the personnel. It is difficult to state what such an improvement means, apart from reducing the delay in court.

Numerical stagnation among the judiciary and the relatively modest growth in the number of cases might suggest that the frequency of conflicts has remained relatively stable. However, this appears unlikely. Industrialization and urbanization must have led to a large increase in the probability of conflicts between citizens and between citizens and public agencies. It is possible, however, that some of the most intensive human conflicts – conflicts that are particularly difficult to solve through negotiations – occurred less frequently. Certain types of religious or sexual misdemeanour that were punished at one time, for example, are now free from penalty, and it may also be the case, with respect to disputes over real estate between farmers in a rural community, that conflicts take a today somewhat different form.

Another, and more likely, explanation of the modest expansion of the personnel and workload of the courts has to do with the growth of legislation and of legal personnel outside the courts. There has been a shift of emphasis from conflict resolution to the prevention of conflicts, or at least the prevention of disputes. The growth of legislation and delegated legislation may have led to the clarification of many legal issues that were previously left unsolved. The increasing formalization of rules has made the outcome of suits more predictable and has thereby encouraged conformity to rules and made it easier to reach settlements out of court.

The growth of a large public bureaucracy recruited by lawyers may also have had a similar effect, though bureaucratic growth and the extension of public intervention may have precipitated large numbers of new disputes. However, these are not in all respects similar to the older conflicts, which arose in connection with crimes or disputes over property and private contracts. The growth of legal expertise in large private firms may also have had the consequence that legal precautions are being taken in advance to prevent later disputes (for example, over contracts).

Disagreements that are finally settled in courts concern, very often, the meting out of penalties. In recent years methods of settling such questions have become more detached from the traditional legal model of applying rules to establish guilt of a certain magnitude. Psychiatric and psychological considerations may intervene, as may predictions concerning the probable effects of a penalty. This new flexibility of trial methods has introduced new opportunities for tacit bargaining. Suspended sentences have become frequent, usually granted on the condition that the defendant fulfils certain requirements, such as paying damages to the victim, abstaining from alcohol, getting a job or maintaining contact with some kind of welfare agency. The judge may let his sentence be influenced by the credibility of the promises made by the defendant and by the arguments advanced in this respect by the counsel for the defence.

Today a large number of cases are being resolved outside the courts, especially outside the more time-consuming and thorough judicial procedures, and the methods of the courts have been changing. This trend can be observed in many different areas. Disputes that originate in taxation or pension claims are normally handled by administrative bodies, although their methods may be more or less reminiscent of judicial ones. In areas like insurance and the building trade, and in other commercial relationships between firms, disputes are settled through private arbitration. Child welfare boards handle the largest number of juvenile delinquencies and other types of conflict between parents and children. With respect to alcohol the temperance boards have been assigned much of the task of conflict resolution in Norway.

In 1814 Norwegian lawyers could be divided into three roughly equal groups: judges, advocates and civil servants in regional administration. In the central administration there were very few lawyers at that time. However, practically all lawyers were in government service, since advocates were civil servants until 1848.

The internal changes that have taken place in the legal profession since 1814 may be summarized in two ways. The private sector of law, represented by advocates and lawyers in business, has grown enormously. Furthermore, there has been a marked increase in the number of lawyers within the central public bureaucracy. Of these two contradictory trends privatization was the dominant one until about 1930. Since then the expansion of the central administration and its legal personnel has been the dominant trait. Parallel to this, there has also been a growth in municipal, county and governmental regional administration.

While the number of judges only doubled during 150 years, the number of advocates increased by a factor of 15. This may well be symptomatic of a change in modes of conflict resolution and of the tendency to solve more legal problems out of court. Advocates have probably taken over much of that function, which consists in the prevention of disputes through counselling and the settlement of conflicts through negotiation. In this context, however, it must not be forgotten that a large number of lawyers in private practice spend most of their time on work that like conveyancing, is only remotely related to the prevention or settlement of conflicts.

It ought to be noted that the distribution of lawyers between different tasks, as it may be observed in Norway, has no universal validity. In Germany the judiciary absorbs a much larger proportion of legally trained people. In other respects there are many similarities between the legal professions in the two countries. In the United States the judiciary absorbs few lawyers, as is the case in Norway. On the other hand, private legal practice predominates, at the expense of government service and private employment, and exhibits in this respect a great difference from the Norwegian pattern.[4]

In any event, in Norway the relative number of law students in the total student population has decreased markedly throughout this century. Around the turn of the century law students were the largest group at the University. Since then the number of engineers, natural scientists, humanists and, in some periods, medical students has exceeded that of the law students. In terms of high-school grades, which give us our only opportunity for a comparison, law students have never excelled. In recent years their grades have declined indicating that the problems of recruitment may be more serious than the numbers indicate.

The scientific basis of most of the professions has expanded constantly throughout this century. Law has not participated to any significant extent in this development, either in terms of research or in terms of teaching. In 1840 there were four permanent teachers of law at the University. In 1940 there were six only, a number which in 1969, however, had increased to thirty. Between

1930 and 1959 there were twelve doctors' degrees in law, as against 210 in medicine, 128 in the humanities, ninety-five in natural science and thirty-two in theology. The deviant position of law in this context is related to its peculiar methods and the nature of knowledge in the field of law. The borderline between research and practice is rather vague.

The trend that emerges from these fragments of legal development is not unequivocal. It is impossible to draw any definite conclusion with respect to the question of whether the legal approach was 'needed' more in the last century than it is now. That law and lawyers had a more dominant role in the last century, and that the scope of the application of the juridical approach was wider, seems to be established, however. This means that as society has changed, the economy has grown; the division of labour has increased; and tasks that were previously assigned to lawyers (and new tasks) have been assigned to other professions and experts.

Alternative modes of dealing with conflicts

The one type of task in which 'loss of functions' is most apparent in the data presented is conflict resolution or, to be more modest and neutral, the *handling* of conflicts. It is, of course, impossible to catalogue all the fora and social settings in which conflicts are dealt with or settled. Some social arrangements are, however, more obviously alternatives to adjudication than others and can be singled out for further analysis. One may divide the relevant agencies roughly into three groups.

The first group takes shape as a form of self-judgment. An organization may offer formal procedures for handling complaints and conflicts that arise between members or between a member and the organization. This occurs in private organizations – for example, through a committee of the Press Association where ethical grievances are considered. Similar procedures are to be found in lawyers' and doctors' associations. Equally, within the governmental apparatus one can find a number of bodies that handle grievances arising out of conflicts between citizens and the state. Such agencies are to be found within tax administration and the pension system; similarly, there are special bodies to handle complaints about government employment (recruitment, promotion, dismissal, etc.). The Ombudsman has something in common with these self-judging agencies, although his position is more independent.

The second category of agencies handles conflicts between the individual and society in a vaguer sense. Here it is frequently a question more of a reaction to deviance than of a dispute between parties. Temperance and child welfare boards provide examples of this type of institution.

The third group of agencies deals with conflicts between parties who otherwise have no links with the agency. They include various arbitration boards, permanent or ad hoc, mediators in labour and other disputes, Prices and Incomes boards. The Labour Court and the Conciliation Boards are formally organized as courts in Norway but have much in common with the other agencies in this group.

Motives for choosing extra-judicial means of dealing with conflict

The emergence and growth of these agencies can, to a certain extent, be seen as a consequence of features of the judicial approach that deter parties from the use of traditional litigation. We shall look briefly at some of these.

The wish of the parties to retain control: the mini-max principle

In chapter 4 we emphasized the all-or-nothing character of legal decisions, albeit tempered by subsidiary considerations. When parties opt for litigation, referring the conflict to a court, this implies that one of the parties may risk a maximal loss. This is an eventuality which most people want to guard themselves against in accordance with the mini-max principle, as it has been termed in the theory of games.[5] Because of the dichotomous nature of legal thinking, the absence of a probabilistic approach, disputing parties have a strong incentive to avoid the courts and either to solve their problems through a dyadic negotiation or to choose a triadic arrangement under which compromise solutions are still possible.

The mini-max principle points to objective realities, to what may actually happen with respect to the distribution of the values at issue. However, the adjudicative model has another aspect of a moral-psychological kind. The judge is obliged to reveal past facts, the history of the case, implying a distribution of guilt, blame and merit. This may intensify the conflict, and it may leave one of the parties, sometimes both, with a blemished self-image.

The Japanese lawyer and sociologist Kawashima has drawn attention to this point in an attempt to explain why the Japanese avoid litigation before a court. He notes that the number of lawyers is relatively low in relation to the size of the population and the level of economic development, indicating that there is no great demand for their services. Likewise, statistics support the notion that disputing parties prefer mediation to adjudication. Kawashima presents the hypothesis that there is something specifically Japanese about this situation and that it must be explained in terms of the social structure and the cultural tradition of Japanese society:

> Traditionally, the Japanese people prefer extra-judicial, informal means of settling a controversy. Litigation presupposes and admits the existence of a dispute and leads to a decision which makes clear who is right or wrong in accordance with standards that are independent of the wills of the disputants. Furthermore, judicial decisions emphasize the conflict between the parties, deprive them of participation in the settlement, and assign a moral fault which can be avoided in a compromise solution.[6]

What Kawashima refers to in this important statement is not applicable only to Japan. He points to motives and considerations that are found generally, although they may have greater force in Japan than in Europe. It should also be noticed that the publicity surrounding adjudication may increase the damage done. For example, in matrimonial cases involving questions of custody, the husband's counsel may see fit to blacken the character of the wife in an attempt to serve his client's interests. Even though unsuccessful, such styles of pleading before a court may do considerable damage and may lead to a loss of confidence and respect among those who get to know about the proceedings. In some cases mediation in the judges's chambers may ameliorate this situation even if adequate means of dispute resolution were not available at an earlier stage.

Kawashima mentions the Japanese preference for boards of mediation. In Europe mediation has probably fulfilled its most useful function in labour disputes, some of which involve questions about wage levels that one could hardly see being handled by legal methods. However, questions that could conceivably have been dealt with by a court have also been settled through mediation or arbitration. Arbitration often resembles adjudication in the sense that it is frequently administered by legal personnel, even judges, who proceed in ways similar to those applied by the courts. The preference for arbitration is rooted primarily in different kinds of consideration, to which I shall return. But one cannot overlook the possibility that arbitration at least appears to allow compromise solutions, since both parties may select representatives to the board of arbitration.[7]

The wish of public agencies and organizations to retain control

We may look upon the preference for internal conflict-solving devices as an asymmetrical extension of consideration A. A governmental agency will often face a demand for remedial procedures when clients feel aggrieved by unfavourable decisions of the agency. From the point of view of the agency, it may seem expedient to establish such procedures within its own purview. This might prevent the occurrence of the harsh, one-sided and public condemnation of its decisions that could occasionally be expected were the grievance to be handled by a regular court completely independent of the agency. From the point of view of the agency's clientele, this advantage may be less apparent. However, such methods of handling complaints may offer them better opportunities for bargaining and thereby retaining some control of the situation. Such is the case with respect to complaints about taxation. When the tax authorities are contemplating filing charges against a tax-payer there may be advantages on both sides to having the issue dealt with by administrative agencies without any publicity. For the tax authorities it can be advantageous to be relieved of the strict judicial requirements concerning evidence. For the tax-payer the relative confidentiality of administrative procedures may seem preferable to the publicity of the court room.

The need for non-legal expertise

The legal model requires that considerable attention be paid to past events, while there is rather limited opportunity to take the possible future consequences of the verdict into consideration. In order to orient decisions towards the future, expertise other than that of the lawyer is called for. In certain types of judicial proceeding there are openings to allow other experts into court or to use them as witnesses. In certain types of criminal case, for example, psychiatrists are included as members of the team that actually makes the decision. However, the need for non-legal expertise and the application of a future-oriented utilitarian model of decision-making has prompted the establishment of a variety of bodies comprising experts from a number of fields.

Boards of arbitration have already been mentioned. One important aspect of many arbitrators is their expertise in a field other than the law, be it the mathematics of insurance, or the problems of the building industry, or industrial relations. It should be mentioned here, however, that many lawyers, whether through training or through experience, acquire expertise in diverse fields and develop a certain ability to think systematically in terms of future consequences.

Family counselling can hardly be seen as an outgrowth of legal institutions, rooted as it is in psychiatric and psychological knowledge and skills. However, family counselling can be seen as a mode of handling conflicts within the family that may serve as an alternative to divorce proceedings and legal battles over custody.

In child welfare and temperance boards much emphasis has been placed on the need both for medical and psychological expertise and for democratic representation. Although these boards do actually intervene in conflicts in families and communities, their attention has tended to focus on the child or the alcoholic as presenting an individualized problem. Clients are defined as deviants, but deviants who are in need of care and not, primarily, disciplinary action. Their role definition is not unlike that attached to the defendant in criminal cases in which psychiatric evidence is of decisive importance.

There is a connection between the intervention of experts with a causal and means—end approach to problem-solving and the definition of the problem as a case of deviance rather than as a conflict. Conflicts require a legal apparatus, the mode of reasoning and decision-making that is adapted to the role of the third party, as shown in chapters 3 and 4. When the cause of the trouble can be located in one individual and the contemplated reaction can be construed as aid, care or therapy, the need to abide by the rule of law seems to evaporate. It is not, apparently, a question of assigning guilt or blame, nor of settling a dispute between two parties. The problem has its immediate cause in the individual himself, even if he may be viewed as a mediator of further problems in his social environment.

Whether this construction is adequate and correct in a deeper sense is often very doubtful. What is viewed as aid and cure by the authorities is frequently resented by the client as unwelcome interference, degradation or deprivation. And what may be presented to the psychiatrist or psychologist as an individual's problem may in reality be no more than one aspect of an interpersonal network, usually a family, in severe unbalance.

In Norwegian legal culture there has been resistance to the establishment of specialized courts in areas where there has appeared to be both a need for and a demand for other kinds of expertise. This is one reason why the so-called Pension Court (the label notwithstanding) has been formally organized outside the judiciary. This court handles a very large number of complaints made by people who feel that they have been deprived of aid to which they are entitled. Since decisions here are of a discretionary nature – to be assessed by specialists in social medicine and related fields – mixed professional backgrounds characterize the members of this court agency.

Time and money

Litigation is time-consuming, and it may also be expensive. It was pointed out in chapter 2 that demands for the strict application of the technically best legal methods can defeat the very aims of the rule of law. The costs and the loss of time may hit different categories of clients unequally; but they may often cause problems for all those who are involved. Conflict-resolving arrangements outside the judiciary have circumvented these difficulties. One important reason why boards of arbitration have been established, and are being preferred to actions before courts, is that they can make quick and cheap decisions. For banks or insurance companies it may even be an advantage to have a quick adverse decision rather than waiting, maybe for years, for their views to be confirmed by a court. Certainty may be more important than sophisticated nuances in the interpretation of the legal situation.

Legal procedures are costly from the point of view of disputing parties; they also constitute a burden upon the public purse. There are reasons why governments find it difficult to justify increasing public expenditure on the court system. As a public service the courts, as mentioned above, hold out no promise that the general welfare of the population will be increased if there is an expansion of the judiciary.

Arbitration seems to be the main time- and money-saving device within civil law. And in criminal cases an option of a fine in lieu of prosecution or the establishment of police courts with summary proceedings similarly cuts costs and time for the police as well as for the accused. Also, administrative agencies with conflict-solving functions may generally dispose of cases more quickly and more cheaply than the judiciary.

Secrecy

Legal procedures are, in principle, open to public inspection and review. This is an aspect of litigation and prosecution that is intimately associated with the rule of law. Since there are conflicts, not least conflicts between the state and the citizen, there has been a demand for openness, for public access to the handling of cases and the reasons given for verdicts. Supposedly this would constitute a guarantee against penalties imposed, or adverse decisions reached, on flimsy or illegal grounds. Unlike the situation in the medical doctor's office, one cannot assume a harmony of interests.

However, the cogency of the two main reasons for this insistent demand for public access to trials and other court proceedings has appreciably declined in many Western countries in recent times. Fear of prosecution on political grounds was a moving factor during and after the period of Enlightenment; political trials now play an insignificant role in most of the countries of the West, although future trends are hard to predict. Closely related to this factor was distrust of the government, a consequence of the prevalence of corruption, as well as the opportunity of the king and his advisors to exert influence upon the judges.

It has already been pointed out that in many normal cases the interests of the parties favour secret deliberation and decision. In criminal cases this can be achieved by holding the proceedings in camera when sensitive evidence is being presented to the court (for example, in trials involving sexual crimes or espionage). Otherwise, those agencies that are set up with the intent of saving time and money usually also offer more confidential treatment of problems than the courts. And this is, no doubt, an important reason for their attraction.

Rationality and irrationality in litigation

Underlying our presentation of reasons for preferring an alternative conflict-solving device, there is the assumption of rationality on the part of the actors. It is rational to act in accordance with the mini-max principle, to save time and money, to shun publicity. However, this assumption of rationality is not always realistic; nor is it always correct to look upon the individual actor as a separate entity, free from ties to other actors. The following remarks refer to the needs and demands of potential court clients, not to the purposes of institutions.

In the course of the development of a grave conflict one of the parties, or both, may come to loathe the mention of any solution that smacks of compromise or presupposes negotiations and contact with the aim of reaching a voluntary settlement. It may be hostility and aggression that make the prospect of such a procedure unpleasant, or the motive may have more to do with self-defence. One party feels righteous, perceives the issue in black-and-white terms, feels that any admission that litigation might lead to loss is onerous and would indicate a flaw in his own moral self-confidence. Prediction of what the courts might decide in fact cannot be separated subjectively from the moral problem of right and justification. In such a situation it is difficult to be a pure positivist. Moral self-righteousness will go hand in hand with an over-estimation of the probability of an affirmative verdict. How well the courts are suited to satisfy those who thirst for justice in this sense may be debatable, but it is easy to see that the courts may attract certain people who harbour moral aggression or need support for their moral defences.

Rationality is a difficult concept. Unusual steps may appear irrational because they are unsuited to furthering the welfare of the actor in the conventional sense. However, an actor may be prompted by a desire to realize unusual values, for the achievement of which these apparently irrational means are suitable. Arson may be a suitable means to satisfy the needs of a pyromaniac. In the present context we look upon rationality in relation to the conventional goals associated with material welfare.

There are conflicts or problems that, by legal stipulation, can be settled only by courts. An important group of criminal cases falls in this category. Some civil suits are instigated because this is the only way in which a change in a certain legal situation can be achieved. Actions to obtain a declaration of legal incompetence fall into this category.

Somewhat related to these cases are actions instigated by civil servants, other kinds of public functionaries, as well as people entrusted with the protection of the interests of private organizations. When embezzlement, for example, takes place in such contexts, those who represent the agency or organization in question may feel bound to report the case to the police even in circumstances in which the party who has suffered loss might see his interests best served by a settlement out of court. Similar considerations may prevent a settlement out of court in civil disputes involving collectivities. The actor is not free to dispose of the matter in the light of his own estimate of what would be best suited to furthering the interests of his organization.

For those who represent organizations another consideration may intervene, namely, a desire for predictability. An insurance company, for example, may in certain circumstances be particularly interested in the authoritative settlement of an ambiguous legal situation. If it wins, its gain transcends the concrete case. If it loses, it may be able to pass any future loss on to its customers by increasing its premiums. It is more advantageous for a 'repeat-player'[8] to risk the hazards of litigation than for those who may appear in court only once in a lifetime. In short, there may be situations in which the choice of litigation may be irrational for organizations, in violation of the mini-max principle and other practical considerations in the individual case, while holding out a promise of a pay-off in the long run.

Individuals who are free to dispose of a dispute on their own, and for whom the dispute is not a recurrent event, may nevertheless feel inclined to opt for litigation out of considerations similar to those that prompt civil servants to propose litigation. Although they are formally free to choose procedure, others (members of the disputant's family, partners, colleagues or neighbours) may be affected by the settlement of the dispute. An agreed compromise may appear to be a sell-out and may give rise to criticism. A loss inflicted by a judicial decision is an authoritative statement of what the plaintiff's rights are and are not.

Socio-legal studies as a means of evaluating the function of law

In the preceding the trend towards the use of legal as against other procedures has been interpreted as evidence of the success and failure of the courts and of legal reasoning to meet individual and societal demands. This represents a functionalist approach, with all the pitfalls involved in such a method, even if the functionalism involved here is of a rather modest kind. No question of societal survival has been raised.

To what extent can empirical sociological evidence provide a basis for the normative evaluation of legal institutions? The value criteria cannot be provided by socio-legal studies, but they might conceivably tell us about the degree to which various legal institution produce decisions and social consequences that are in accordance with the publicly announced ideals of justice. Prominent among these ideals is equality before the law.

By now an impressive number of empirical studies have been undertaken with the aim of revealing hidden patterns in judicial decisions, patterns determined by factors that are, strictly speaking, legally irrelevant. These studies rely on a comparative method. They present comparisons either of individual judges and jurisdictions or of groups of clients, defendants or parties in civil suits. In order to draw evaluative conclusions from such studies, one must have good reasons to assume that the cases dealt with, whether from the point of view of the court personnel or of the clientele, are equal with respect to legally relevant criteria. However, the difficulty of separating these factors from those that do not, in theory, have legal relevance, has proved a stumbling-block in many such studies. To the extent that inequalities are registered, the question may arise of whether these indicate inequality *before* the law or *in* the law.

Uniformity and variation in law enforcement

The first study known to me was the one conducted by Everson in the police courts of New York. Finding striking disparities in the sentencing patterns of the magistrates covered by the study, he concluded: 'justice is a very personal thing.'[9] A study conducted in Canada fifty years later produced results that prompted the author to conclude his report with the very same words.[10] Between these two studies a large number of research reports seem to prove that a personal element does indeed intrude into the decision-making process on the bench. Whether it is justified to claim that justice is a '*very* personal thing' must remain a moot point.

At first glance some of these studies may seem to support one of the basic tenets of the American school of legal realism, jokingly called 'breakfast jurisprudence', which refers to the possibility that the judge's mood may be influenced by idiosyncratic factors, like the quality of his breakfast. However, most of the empirical studies do not go beyond the mere registration of variation between judges. The causation and motivation of such variance must remain more or less guesswork.[11]

In some of the studies individual variations seem to be of a systematic nature, rooted in an adherence to different legal or political ideologies that are not, strictly speaking, entirely personal. This is true of the systematic and disparate voting patterns that Pritchett[12] and later Schubert[13] discovered among the justices of the US Supreme Court. In some other studies the comparison covers judicial personnel of different categories, such as professional judges versus jurors or lay judges.[14] Their sentencing tendencies also exhibit systematic differences.

How are we to evaluate the fact that judges vary in the sentences they hand down? Variations may be due to three different factors or mechanisms. First, they may be rooted in methodological error, in that the researcher has not succeeded in allowing for all legally relevant factors. If that is so, variation may be caused by an unequal selection of cases among judges. This source of error is especially likely to occur when different jurisdictions are compared. In studies of dissenting votes in a collegiate court, the comparability of cases is more or less guaranteed.

Second, the disparities may be regarded as random variations around a norm. Their scope will then be decisive for the normative evaluation of the patterns revealed. If their scope is limited, there may be no detraction from the aim of securing predictability for the citizens. Predictions are hardly very accurate anyway. Unfortunately, behavioural studies of the judiciary often fail to give an indication of the magnitude of the variations, even when this is measurable. Frequently the magnitude is not measurable, since the decisions take an either/or form. Then we have to take into consideration the fact that the court cases are unrepresentative of the total universe of potential disputes, most of which are settled out of court. They may comprise problems that are particularly complex and uncertain, and this may contribute to variation in judicial practice.

Third, judicial variation may be explained by the systematic interference of factors outside of the recognized sources of law. Nagel found that the political party allegiance of judges was associated with their sentencing behaviour, especially when they did not have tenure.[15] This is possibly the most serious signal of a breach with the rule of law to be gleaned from the empirical studies of judicial behaviour. The main reason for concern is not the systematic variation as such, however. It is rather that once we know about the susceptibility of judges to influence from political allegiance, social background and pressures, we must ask some further questions.

Could it also be that uniformity in judicial practice may be caused by factors that go beyond the recognized sources of law? Could it be that the law is interpreted by a corpus of lawyers who have a relatively uniform social background and social and political ideology (in spite of varying party preference) and are exposed to a similar educational and professional environment? Studies of recruitment to the legal profession and to the judiciary suggest that judges are far from representative of the population with respect to social background.[16]

What I want to suggest is that variation as such is less important than the causes of variation. Through the analysis of cases we may start to identify very general factors that may subvert the legislator's attempts to guide or direct the enforcement of the law. Now, the existence of a judiciary independent of the executive as well as of legislative power has been considered a cornerstone of the ideology of the rule of law. Empirical studies of judicial behaviour raise, by implication, some doubts about the effectiveness of the guarantees offered by the courts if they are dependent upon outside social forces. In countries with a wide gap between social classes or ethnic groups this dependence may be a serious problem. Uniformity in judicial behaviour may in such circumstances be no great sign of health in the law. Some deviant judgments might actually constitute an improvement in terms of a wider conception of justice and the rule of law.

If we consider the total process of law enforcement, the most important sources of variation, exhibiting the highest susceptibility to outside and irrelevant factors, are not to be found in the courts. The police and the prosecuting agencies are granted rather wide discretionary powers by the law. It seems from some studies that the use of these powers is determined in a systemic fashion by motives and pressures that cannot be accounted for by reference to the law or to legal doctrine.[17] This fact has to do with the economy of sanctions and the scarcity of resources that characterize the administration of justice. It is in the stages prior to trials that the basic selection and sampling of cases takes place. Since the law cannot admit explicitly that there must be such a selection, nor can it establish priorities in police work.

Equality before the courts

Some of these problems are raised even more conspicuously by studies that compare the fate of different groups of clients who appear before the courts. We shall focus here upon those studies that give the impression that the outcome of a case depends to a greater or lesser extent upon the social status of the client, especially in criminal actions. The methodological problems that confront the researcher in this area are formidable, however, and many studies are inconclusive.[18]

To illustrate the problems involved and the possible conclusions to be drawn, I shall report, in summary form, on one of my own studies.[19] It comprises the criminal cases dealt with by six District Courts over a period of ten years, 2083 in all. The defendants were grouped on the basis of an index of social status, combining occupation and income. When all the cases were divided according to the status of the defendant, a tabular presentation of the outcome of the cases revealed enormous disparities between the status groups. Members of the lowest-status groups were almost never acquitted and most received quite a heavy prison sentence. At the other end of the social scale a complete reversal of this trend appeared. Thirty-nine per cent of this high-status or middle-class group were acquitted, and only 2 per cent of them received light prison sentences. Between these two extremes the defendants belonging to various status groups distributed themselves according to a fairly neat pattern.

Controls were then introduced, first the division of the clientele according to the type of crime involved. This showed, not surprisingly, that defendants of different social status are charged with different types of crime, or rather show different profiles with respect to the distribution of charges. High-status people were charged disproportionately often with traffic violation, whereas the normal procedure is that the offender accepts a writ in lieu of prosecution and pays the fine. The cases that appear in court at the behest of the accused constitute a biased sample, with heavy representation of doubtful cases and of defendants with social resources and self-confidence. Given these circumstances, it is to be expected that the rate of acquittal should be high.

Similar factors operate to determine variations in the penalties imposed according to social status. There is some irregularity in the distribution of social status categories between types of offence. For fourteen crime categories the material was divided into first offenders and recidivists. Within most of these twenty-eight categories of offenders there was a difference between those with very low social status and those with an average or higher social status, biased in favour of the latter, although the difference rarely reached the level of statistical significance. The clearest difference was found among the thieves. Some further controls were introduced, but figures dwindled so as to prevent reliable statistical inference.

The pattern that emerged from this study was the following. In a global analysis, in which all kinds of crime are indiscriminately combined, status differences are glaring. These differences diminish considerably when the material is grouped by type of offence. They are further reduced when previous criminal record is introduced as a control by dividing the material into first offenders and recidivists. One might speculate about what would happen if the material had permitted further subdivision as a result of including new factors that, according to precedent and prevailing theory, are legally relevant. It is conceivable that the social differences would then disappear completely, although this does not seem likely.

In such an analysis we would end up with some queries about what is and what is not a legally relevant criterion. To the extent that the criminal law permits or encourages courts to embark upon a policy of resocialization and individual prevention, factors associated with social status, such as position on the labour market, at school and with respect to family and home, may become relevant to the choice of penalty. The possession of some resources may operate to the advantage of one defendant so that he will be set free on probation, while another, totally dispossessed defendant would receive an unconditional sentence. Would this represent the strict application of the law or a moderation of it based upon criteria external to the legal system?

A Swedish study puts this question into perspective in a paradoxical way. It was found that the magistrate's decision was correlated more closely with traditional criteria for the imposition of punishment (gravity of offence, recidivism, etc.) than it was with social criteria, like poverty, unemployment, housing situation, family status. This statistical pattern was interpreted as breaching the intentions of the legislator in instituting a system of rules based upon the aims of individual prevention and resocialization. What in other studies would be considered a deviation from the principle of equality before the law would here have been interpreted as a sign of faithful adherence to the law.[20]

This study, as well as the above demonstration of the reduction of inequalities by the introduction of legal controls in tabular analysis, may point to a more important inequality, that embedded in the law itself. When inequalities between status categories are systematically reduced by the subdivision of defendants into groups ever more narrowly defined in terms of the legally relevant criteria, all these criteria are closely associated with social status. That the law tends to protect the haves against the have nots is no new discovery, but it may be of interest to see the principle demonstrated by these methodological devices.

To the ambiguities surrounding the question of what constitutes inequality before the law is added another source of reassurance that all is well with law and law enforcement: the philosophically underpinned notion that the law is what the courts do. An individual judge may occasionally stray from the fold, but the judiciary as a whole can, by positivist definition, do no wrong. The judiciary enjoys a kind of philosophical protection against serious criticism, probably merging with a popular need for assurance that somewhere in a bewildering threatening social environment there exists one infallible and benevolent authority.

Whether empirical studies of judicial behaviour are interpreted in terms of inequality before the law or in the law, they throw some new light upon the practical implications of the rule of law. The value of the protection of rights offered by the courts, *vis-à-vis* the government, depends upon the magnitude of the rights of those who are offered such protection. The rule of law, narrowly and juridically construed, does not imply that the courts should create new rights for those who suffer from legal deficiencies. The rule of law protects the *status quo*. No doubt this may be of some benefit to underprivileged groups, but it is even more advantageous for those who are already well equipped with rights.[21]

This point may be clearly demonstrated by studies of access to the law (usually meaning access to legal services in the form of legal counsel, lawyers and barristers), which appears to be very unequally distributed according to the socio-economic status of the clientele.[22] When this is explained by lack of economic resources, inadequate information, fear of lawyers and so on, the defensive answer is that it is perfectly natural that the haves should use lawyers more than the have nots because they have more legal problems to cope with. This is hardly a satisfactory explanation. However, to the extent that it contains a kernel of truth, the implication is that the haves possess more rights to protect. Since access to legal counsel is an important element in practical actions and as an aid in the course of litigation, unequal access to legal services means that this principle does not benefit the population indiscriminately and regardless of social status. Like so much else in the law, the very principle of the rule of law is class-bound.

Notes

1 In accordance with common Scandinavian terminology, I use the term 'lawyer' about anyone with a law degree, whether he practises law as an advocate, serves as a judge or occupies a position in public or private administration. No one without a degree has been permitted to practise law in Norway during the period we are concerned with here.
2 Cf. Ralf Dahrendorf, 'The education of an elite: law faculties and the German upper class', *Transactions of the Fifth World Congress of Sociology* (Louvain: 1964), vol. 3, pp. 259–74.
3 James S. Coleman, 'The methods of sociology', in Robert Bierstedt (ed.), *A Design for Sociology: Scope, Objectives, and Methods* (Philadelphia: American Academy of Political and Social Science, 1969).
4 Cf. Dietrich Rüschemeyer, *Lawyers and Their Society. A Comparative Study of the Legal Profession in Germany and in the United States* (Cambridge, Mass.: Harvard University Press, 1973).
5 Cf. chapter 2, note 36.
6 Takeyoshi Kawashima, 'Dispute resolution in contemporary Japan', in Arthur Taylor von Mehren (ed.), *Law in Japan. The Legal Order of a Changing Society* (Cambridge, Mass.: Harvard University Press and Charles F. Tuttle, 1964), p. 43. See also Dan Fenno Henderson, *Conciliation and Japanese Law, Tokugawa and Modern* (Seattle/Tokyo: University of Washington Press, 1965), esp. pp. 235ff.
7 Britt-Mari Blegvad, P.O. Bolding, Ole Lando and Kirsten Gamst-Nielsen, *Arbitration as a Means of Solving Conflicts,* New Social Science Monographs E6 (Copenhagen: 1973), p. 117.
8 Marc Galanter, 'Why the "haves" come out ahead: speculations on the limits of legal change', *Law and Society Review,* 9 (1974), pp. 95–160.
9 George Everson, 'The human element in justice'. *Journal of Criminal Law, Criminology and Police Science,* 10 (1919–20), p. 90.
10 John Hogarth, *Sentencing as a Human Process* (Toronto: University of Toronto Press, 1971), p. 365.
11 An attempt to relate behaviour on the bench to personality factors can be found in Harold Lasswell, *Power and Personality* (New York: Norton, 1948).
12 C. Herman Pritchett, *The Roosevelt Court: a Study in Judicial Politics and Values, 1937–47* (New York: Macmillan, 1948); *Civil Liberties and the Vinson Court* (Chicago: University of Chicago Press, 1954).
13 Glendon Schubert, *Quantitative Analysis of Judicial Behavior* (New York: Free Press, 1959).
14 Harry Kalven Jr and Hans Zeisel, *The American Jury* (Boston/Toronto: Little, 1966). Vilhelm Aubert, *Likhet og rett* (Equality and the Law) (Oslo: Pax Forlag, 1964), pp. 144ff.
15 Stuart S. Nagel, 'Political party affiliation and judges' decisions'. *American Political Science Review* (1961), pp. 843ff.

16 Vilhelm Aubert, *Rettens sosiale funksjon* (The Social Function of Law) (Oslo/Bergen/Tromsø: Universitetsforlaget, 1976), p. 232. Cf. also Vilhelm Aubert, 'The professions in Norwegian social structure', *Transactions of the Fifth World Congress of Sociology,* International Sociological Association (1964), Table 2, pp. 256–7; German data in Ralf Dahrendorf, 'Deutsche Richter. Ein Beitrag zur Soziologie der Oberschict', in *Gesellschaft und Freiheit* (Munich: R. Piper, 1962), pp. 176–96; Wolfgang Kaupen, *Die Hüter von Recht und Ordnung* (Neuwied/Berlin: Luchterhand, 1969), pp. 103, 135.

17 Jerome Skolnick, *Justice Without Trial: Law Enforcement in Democratic Society* (New York: John Wiley, 1966); Abraham Blumberg, *Criminal Justice* (Chicago: Quadrangle, 1967).

18 Cf., for example, Frederick Joseph Gaudet, 'Individual differences in the sentencing tendencies of judges', *Archives of Psychology,* 230 (New York: 1938); Sam Bass Warner and Henry B. Cabot, *Judges and Law Reform* (Cambridge, Mass.: Harvard University Press, 1936); Matthew F. McGuire, and Alexander Holzhoff, 'The problem of sentencing in the criminal law', *Boston University Law Review,* 413, pp. 724–33; W. E. von Eyben, *Strafudmåling* (The Meting out of Punishment) (Copenhagen: G. E. C. Gads, 1950.) Edward Green, *Judicial Attitudes in Sentencing* (London: Macmillan, 1961). Herbert Jacob and James Eisenstein, 'Sentences and other sanctions in the criminal courts of Baltimore, Chicago, and Detroit', *Political Science Quarterly,* 90 (1975), pp. 617–35; Roger Hood, *Sentencing in Magistrates' Courts* (London: Stevens 1962), esp. pp. 118–27; excerpt in Vilhelm Aubert (ed.), *Sociology of Law,* (Harmondsworth: Penguin, 1969), pp. 228–36. Cf. also references in Lawrence M. Friedman and Stuart Macauly, *Law and the Behavioral Sciences,* 2nd edn. (Indianapolis/New York: Bobbs-Merrill, 1977).

19 Aubert, *Likhet og rett,* pp. 130ff.

20 Ulla Bondeson, *Kriminalvård i frihet* (Extra-institutional Correctional Treatment) (Stockholm: Liber Förlag, 1977), p. 140.

21 Ragnhild Øvrelid, 'Forvalningen og almenheten' (The Civil Service and the Public), unpublished manuscript (Oslo: 1981).

22 Aubert, *Rettens sosiale funksjon,* pp. 263ff.; Jerome E. Carlin, *Lawyers' Ethics: A Survey of the New York City Bar* (New York: Russell Sage Foundation, 1966), esp. pp. 177–8; J. E. Carlin and Jan Howard, 'Legal representation and class justice', *UCLA Law Review,* 12 (1965), pp. 381–431; excerpt in Aubert, *Sociology of Law,* pp. 332–50. Cf. also references in Friedman and Macauly, *Law and the Behavioral Sciences,* p. 925.

CHAPTER 7

Human rights and the promotional function of law

In chapters 1 and 2 law was viewed as an attempt to answer fundamental human needs. It was presented to a large extent as an ideology. In subsequent chapters attention was paid to the other side of the Janus face of law — law as a technique for the handling of social problems, especially interpersonal conflicts. The tension between ideology and technique that characterizes the legal scene often takes the form of a gap between the concerns of ordinary people all over the world and the concerns of the Western professional guardians of the niceties of legal technique. The excerpts presented in chapter 2 from the reports of the International Commission of Jurists testify to this gap.

The revival in recent years of natural law, or doctrines with some kinship with natural law, is but one symptom of a new and intensified quest for law, and law in a sense that transcends the positivist approach. The question arises of whether a wide and idealistic conception of law, not simply a minimum standard of conduct, can be maintained without breaking away altogether from the narrower, professional concept of law.

The expansion of law[1]

We shall look now at some of the trends that foster tension between the two approaches and some of the symptoms that indicate that arguments and thinking in terms of natural law are gaining in strength. One very general factor may lie at the root of these trends: the vast increase in recent years in the level of organization in the world, which has occurred on a global scale.

The various countries, regions and continents of the world are increasingly being woven into a close-knit web of economic, political, military and cultural relationships. Concomitantly, new states have arisen out of the ashes of colonial empires, and some old states, such as China, are coming into their own and being consolidated in a new way. The older nation-states of the Western hemisphere have expanded their centralized resources and activities. Simultaneously, their citizens are organized increasingly in a plethora of associations.

Organization implies rules, decision-making and the need for conflict resolution. The application of legal principles and techniques lies near at hand. We see it in its clearest and most traditional form in the growth of legislation within nation-states, old and new. To the extent that this legislation aims at economic development and social welfare, in the widest sense, the guardians of legal technique and the rule of law are faced with new and baffling problems. Law is no longer simply the institutionalized expression of certain minimum standards of conduct, nor merely a framework of rules regulating the otherwise free play of market forces. Legislative acts outline, implicitly or programmatically, the course of future development and a commitment to ideals as yet beyond reach. Direct coercion is no longer the hallmark of legal enforcement.

The vast growth of administrative law, regulating the distribution of resources gathered through increasingly effective taxation, raises new problems with respect to the adherence to the rule of law. The pattern outlined in chapter 2 as a description of the *Rechtsstaat* ideology fragments. A tension emerges between the demands of the rule of law doctrine and the faithful execution of a legal policy that could ensure the realization of ideals underlying, or expressed in, this new legislation.

Acts of Parliament that aim at full equality between the sexes or between racial and ethnic groups, laws that proclaim safety, satisfaction and security in all kinds of employment, the right to work for all able-bodied adults and equal opportunity to receive education for everyone can serve as examples of a trend in much recent legislation. The tendency to include in the law visions of a future ideal state of affairs can be seen as a commitment to a way of thinking that bears some resemblance to the natural law approach. Although programmatic clauses are duly established and promulgated through democratic procedures in accordance with constitutional law, some of them are in practice unenforcable. But this does not necessarily mean that they are empty words without practical consequences: they constitute a basis for reviewing and, if necessary, criticizing the law as applied by the agencies of enforcement. And this basis is of a collective kind, not merely anchored in the moral consciousness of individuals who may object to the way in which the law is put into practice. Behind these types of more or less unenforcable legislative act, lies, of course, a human rights approach. The historical link with the natural law tradition is undeniable.

Two kinds of human rights

Human rights are rights that pertain to individuals simply because they are human.[2] They are, as it were, innate rights, not rights that are acquired through achievement or qualification. In the Western legal tradition (the tradition out of which positivism grew) no right can exist without the imposition of a complementary duty on some other person. In Hohfeld's scheme of basic legal concepts this is a central notion.[3] There is an intimate connection between this construction and the concept of law as representing minimum standards of conduct, as well as the definition of law as a set of coercive rules. 'Duty' is the most basic legal term. 'Right' constitutes a claim that somebody else should fulfil his duty and perform or abstain from interfering.

Those human rights that were instituted as a consequence of the Enlightenment were essentially 'freedom rights', rights to life, liberty, property and the pursuit of happiness. In principle, these rights aimed at creating a core area in every individual's action space from which outside interference was banned. The fact that this protection was in practice very unevenly granted and was long the prerogative only of those who were deemed qualified for full citizenship,[4] need not concern us here, although this limitation has been of the utmost importance. What is of immediate concern here is that these rights presuppose a structure of duties and sanctions against the breach of obligations. The kind of state that could offer such a protective structure was the 'night-watchman's state' and, somewhat later, the law state (*Rechtsstaat*), the latter offering even some protection against its own might.

These kinds of human right presupposed two things: first, as mentioned above, that there existed a superordinate power capable of enforcing duties and, second, that there was something to protect. It was not, on the whole, the duty of the state to create life, property or happiness. The rights were in this sense negative, mirror-images of duties not least the duty of the state powers to leave the citizens alone. As we saw in chapter 2, it was this situation that fostered rule of law ideology. In this early version there was harmony between the rule of law and the quest for the protection of human rights.

This harmony was shattered by Marx's onslaught on bourgeois legal conceptions and the capitalist state. Although Marx and his successors tried to avoid all contamination with concepts of natural law or human rights in any legalistic sense, his theory — and the revolutions executed in his name — paved the way for a much wider concept of human rights. The constitutions of socialist or communist states retain, in principle, the traditional Western 'freedom rights — those of speech, of assembly, *nulla poena sine lege,* even the protection of private property. In addition, these constitutions guarantee their citizens the right to work, health care, education, cultural participation, etc. A catchword for these rights has been 'economic, social and cultural rights' — in essence, the right to a decent life.[5]

In the old law states of the Western world a similar development started before the Russian or Chinese revolutions. The welfare state is one that offers its citizens a positive minimum of welfare, not simply protection of their right to fend for themselves.[6] In a more active form the social democracies of Western Europe hold out a promise that goes beyond the minimum of welfare. As mentioned above, they have started on the process of instituting rights to a good, or at least decent, life. The Swedish Constitution of 1976 (§2) enumerates explicitly the basic goals of the welfare state: the freedom and dignity of the individual, welfare, the right to work, social security, equality between the sexes and protection of the rights of minorities. It has already been noted that the Norwegian Constitution contains a clause that enunciates, in a non-justiciable way, the right to work, but on the whole the Norwegian Constitution limits itself to the protection of the traditional freedom rights.

I cannot deal here with the relationship between ideals and reality, whether in socialist or in capitalist countries. It is quite clear, however, that to draw conclusions about actual living conditions from the presence or absence of formal constitutional protection of human rights of either kind would be grossly misleading. Innumerable violations of human rights have been recorded in countries with impeccable constitutional guarantees of the basic 'freedom rights'. On the other hand, the countries with constitutional provisions to protect economic, social and cultural rights tend not to belong to that part of the world that has the highest per capita income or the highest level of material welfare.

Somewhat reluctantly, the Western countries have come to accept international declarations of human rights that encompass economic, social and cultural aspects of welfare. But they have been hesitant to include protection of such rights in their own constitutions, in spite of the fact that they should be in a better material position than avowed socialist countries to honour the promises contained in such clauses. The chauvinist Western explanation of this reluctance to institute constitutional or other legal guarantees of the good life is that truly democratic states hesitate to mislead even a few of their citizens about what they can expect from the state. The socialist reaction to this might be that the Western countries, even those with a social democratic government, are ruled by the aim of protecting capitalist interests. It is presumably not in the interest of capitalists that welfare should be a guaranteed right of everybody since this would require a massive redistribution of income and would make great inroads into the freedom of the market.[7]

There may be a grain of truth in both of these contentions, the self-appreciative and the critical. The ambivalent attitude of the industrially advanced states of the Western world towards the institutionalization of welfare as a legal right is rooted in an historically given social structure. However, the most readily accessible key to an understanding of the different conceptions of human rights in Western and socialist countries is the confrontation of the differing theories of the state that prevail in these two parts of the world.

Two theories of the state

As mentioned in chapter 2, the Western theory of the state, with its emphasis on the division of powers and the self-limitation of centralized authority, builds upon distrust of any person in a position of political power, however democratically elected. The negligent attitude towards those with private economic power is, as described in chapter 5, a product of the masking of the real relationships in the market by the obsolete legal construction of private property as a nexus between the 'owner' and a 'thing'.

It can be argued, on the other hand, that the unambiguous will to espouse economic, social and cultural rights in socialist constitutions is consistent with the Marxian conception of the harmony of interests that exists between those who govern and those who are governed under communism. We must, then, overlook the original theory of the withering away of the state under communism; it has proved to be wholly unrealistic and has been completely abandoned in practice. Alternatively, one might advance the hypothesis that a state that derives its legitimacy from a theory, one tenet of which is the withering away of the very state itself, thereby affirms its subservience to the people. The state is no more than a temporary evil during the period of transition, the dictatorship of the proletariat.

In order to understand the establishment of constitutional guarantees of economic, social and cultural rights, another aspect of Marxian theory must be taken into account. Poverty and its concomitants are, according to this theory, very largely the consequence of the exploitation of one class by another under a system of private capitalism administered by a bourgeois state. Once the shackles of repressive forces are removed (as similar constraints were removed when capitalism superseded feudalism), well-nigh unlimited progress in the productive forces may be expected, as well as a concomitant increase of human welfare. And since the revolution will have done away with class antagonisms and a state dominated by the interests of one class, the distribution of increasing wealth will raise no serious problems.

Given these ideological premises, there will no longer be any reason for legal soft-pedalling over economic, social and cultural rights. There will be no curb on the urge to put ideals and programmes – in short, a morality of excellence – into legal or even constitutional form. Inexorable social forces will guarantee citizens the satisfaction of their needs, since the cause of poverty and inequality will have been removed. The state of freedom will supersede the state of necessity. The level of welfare may, of course, be modest and resources scarce in the initial stages on the road towards communism. Since this will be merely a residue of the preceding capitalist society, no conflict will arise out of this situation of scarcity and necessity. No responsibility for the temporarily sordid state of affairs will justifiably be assigned to the new revolutionary government; all guilt will be ascribed to the fallen capitalist regime, the new state will be the people's own state, so that the interests of the government will be inseparable from the interests of the people, or at least of the toiling masses. Criticisms of governmental policy will boil down to self-criticism, a type of political activity that plays a role in communist states unknown in Western countries.

It is not easy to present the Western counterpart to these fragments of Marxist-based ideology. Unlike communist constitutions, Western constitutions do not refer explicitly to any consistent political theory, although the Amendments to the United States Constitution are couched in the language of liberal ideology. Underlying Western constitutions, as mentioned already, we can discern distrust of any government, the notion that power corrupts and must be kept under control. Another tenet of Western faith, or that branch of it that has survived in Western Europe in particular, is the belief in scarcity so dramatically espoused by Thomas Malthus at the beginning of the last century. The present movement towards environmental protection is a late outgrowth of this traditional belief and contrasts with the technological optimism of Marx and Lenin and their heirs.

Scarcity, inequality and a certain amount of misery have been viewed as more or less natural aspects of the human condition. In this context the notion that human talent itself is scarce and must be cultivated by differential rewards, upholding social inequality, is important. In short, there is in the background of Western constitutions an inclination to view misery less as a result of social forces than as a product of biological or natural conditions, if not ordained by the will of God.

Among the diffuse theoretical notions that form the background to Western constitutions there is no assumption that progress, liberation from the past, will automatically ensure harmony of interests in society or between the citizens and the government. Democracy means competition for power among political groupings, organized as parties, that with varying degrees of faithfulness express class and other factional interests. This forces the government into a position in which it woos the electorate rather than being the leading section of a larger whole. Even under peaceful and rather stable conditions, the government and the citizenry are viewed as two players, whose communality of interests can never be taken for granted. Equally, the party political system confirms continually that there *are* conflicting interests between groups of citizens.

This conception of state and society makes it risky for any government to make promises about adjudicable rights. More than that, extravagant promises in legal form of increased welfare could jeopardize the whole political system and could threaten the interests of powerful groups in society, in the economy as well as in the polity. The traditional 'freedom rights' lie within the compass of matters directly manipulable by the state organs themselves. I refer to a point of view that was presented in chapter 2 under the discussion of the rule of law ideology. The law state offers certainty with respect to the operation of the state organs themselves, a negative certainty that no harm will be inflicted by the state upon those who obey its laws.

The promotional function of law[8]

The welfare states have gone beyond this conception of the function of law and government with respect to both goal-setting and to technique. In so far as ideas and conscious plans shape policy, the goals are influenced by prevailing notions of human rights. On the technical level there has been a shift from methods of prevention, as advocated by Machiavelli and his successors, to methods of promotion, the use of rewards and encouragement.

Behind this shift of emphasis lies the economic growth of the Western world, to which has been coupled a fairly effective system of taxation. The amassed wealth of modern states has changed the very principles of public governance. The coercive element has receded into the background, while money and other material resources have become the principal means of affecting the lives and behaviour of citizens. It may well be claimed that the basis of the strength of a government is less its ability to punish or deprive its citizens than its ability to satisfy their material needs.[9]

While recognizing the positive, promotional aspect of much modern legislation, there are those who would still maintain that the basic factor underlying the strength of a government and the efficacy of its laws is the availability of means of coercion.[10] It must be admitted that the vast growth in weaponry and in the significance of the military establishment, even in the welfare states, makes it somewhat difficult to claim that the old theory of law, based upon force and coercion, has become wholly obsolete. In other parts of the world under military government it is quite clear that Sohm's definition of law, *sub hasta* (under the spear), remains painfully accurate.[11] In spite of these circumstances, however, the enormous significance of the distribution of resources as a governmental task, regulated by law, calls at least for an amelioration of the Austinian definition.

The fact that the government is using its resources and its legislative powers to promote certain activities and to create situations should not lead us to assume that the welfare or interventionist states are thereby pursuing successfully a consistent programme of social reform. These modern states function in many ways as cafeterias rather than as leading forces in the nations. The government is responsive to an increasing number of claims from ever more vocal and better organized interest groups.[12] Many legal enactments and corresponding actions must be viewed from this perspective rather than as elements in a coherent programme designed to further specific societal goals.

In themselves the wealth of the state and the importance of resource distribution do not imply that the government is using rewards as a technique of motivating people to behave in conformity with certain norms. Medical aid or a disability pension under a public health scheme do not function as rewards for falling ill or for being unfit to work and unable to provide for oneself. Since the individuals and families who tend to receive benefit from these types of income redistribution are, on the whole, understood to be in an unfortunate position, they only occasionally have a motivating effect on other people. By and large, the conditions that legitimize the provision of public support are unrelated to behaviour but, like old age, are considered to be caused by circumstances beyond the individual's control.

The existence of welfare legislation may, however, have a motivating impact upon people who consider immigration to countries practising such systems. Whether the availability of welfare schemes should be viewed as rewards for immigrants or guest workers depends upon the policy of the receiving country. Rarely, if ever, have welfare schemes been devised with the aim of attracting immigrants, guest workers or tourists. The 'rewarding function' of welfare laws is a latent one.

These brief remarks on welfare laws call to our attention the complexity of the system of sanctions in a modern state. We are constantly reminded of this complexity and of the interplay between legal and other social factors when we move on to the more directly promotional aspects of legislation and administrative systems built upon law. We find such systems in the economic, educational, cultural and other spheres of social life. It has been the conscious and emphasized aim of the industrialized, capitalist countries of the world, above all of social democratic governments, to further economic, social and cultural growth, and to do so to a large extent by legislative prescription. However, much governmental aid to all sectors of the economy, from agriculture to electronics, is provided by ad hoc appropriations, and law recedes into the background.

One very clear example of the promotional aspect of law can be found in legislation that establishes criteria and administrative machinery for supplying aid to economically underdeveloped areas of the country in question. Such legislation exists in most West European countries. Norwegian law offers grants, loans, guarantees of loans and certain other services to firms that are established in peripheral and underdeveloped districts. It is quite clear that the intention behind the law is to reward behaviour that may promote economic activity.

Tax exemptions represent other instances of legally instituted rewards for economic behaviour deemed favourable by the government. However, to judge whether a certain level of taxation is to be considered a reward, one has to view the separate clauses of tax law within a wider context. By definition, taxation, even at the lowest level, imposes a burden upon the taxpayer. Yet since a modern society without some taxation is unthinkable, the question of whether a specific tax represents a penalty or a reward must be viewed in a comparative perspective. What kinds of investment of capital or labour are being heavily taxed, and what types of investment are tax exempt or taxed at reduced rates? There can be little doubt that tax reductions and exemptions must be viewed as positive sanctions, as rewards motivating people to act in certain ways and to avoid other courses of action. However, some qualification must be added, namely, that not all of the activities that are, as a matter of fact, rewarded by the tax system, favour the kind of investment that government plans presuppose. The right to deduct interest on any loan in Norway, taken up for whatever purpose, has greatly encouraged investment in luxurious houses, cars and boats for those who have good bank connections. The preservation of such laws must be regarded not simply as a rational effort with a utilitarian aim but as a means of gaining political support from groups with considerable power. If we view the right to deduct interest from income in conjunction with heavy progressive taxation, it is tempting to ascribe to tax law a latent political function. Progressive taxation satisfies the less privileged that the rich pay their share. The right to deduct interests from income alleviates the deprivations inherent in a steep tax progression. Such combinations of more or less contradictory laws testify to the symbolic function of law as expressive of attractive ideals for groups with opposing interests.

Beyond the rule of law

The law state offered the citizen protection against certain misfortunes caused by the state itself or by wilful acts of other citizens. The welfare state offers protection against certain calamities beyond the control of the state or its citizenry, like illness, old age and certain types of unemployment. However, it is still a question of guaranteeing a certain minimum of welfare, increasing predictability and a sense of security but not promising a rose garden. Economic growth has been the precondition for the development of these minimum welfare rights. Increasingly, it has been seen as the government's responsibility to interfere with market forces if this is deemed necessary to secure continued growth or at least to avoid a reduction of the national product. We have seen a few examples of how this aim is achieved through legislation.

Welfare legislation may be viewed as derived directly from conceptions of human rights. Laws that aim at promoting economic growth are, from the point of view of human rights, only instruments, albeit important instruments. In a negative sense, however, this kind of legislation has often been considered a threat to the rule of law and to the procedural guarantees of human rights, to the due process of law. Administrative decisions in this area tend to be discretionary and therefore not readily amenable to judicial review. Since the criteria for awarding aid may be vaguely formulated, doubts may easily arise about there being equality before the law, and as the groups that are affected by such decisions have some standing and power, their protests may create problems. Parallel problems within the welfare sector surface with less force, since the social positions of the groups affected are more peripheral.

The welfare state must respond to three kinds of demand — for minimum welfare benefits and services, for economic growth and for the preservation of the rule of law and traditional 'freedom rights'. Since these claims often clash, it is important to find out how they may be balanced so that the legitimacy and the stability of the state are not seriously threatened. The task is not to discern a scheme for manipulation developed by the political elite but to trace the historical emergence of social arrangements capable of absorbing the ideological tensions caused by conflicting demands.

The separation of social arenas

One key to understanding is the existence of vital social arenas where justice and the rule of law are not considered to be directly applicable and where legal interference is considered impossible or detrimental. The market in the Western welfare states falls into this category.

The government shares responsibility for economic growth with the market. From the government's point of view, an optimal situation might be one in which it exerted sufficiently strict control over the economy to ward off disastrous slumps without appearing to be responsible should such setbacks nevertheless occur. Whatever claims can be made for different kinds of mix in mixed-economy nations, the market is available as an excuse for unemployment, inflation and other mishaps as long as the citizens by and large see some merit in a free market. When it does not deliver the goods, the free market becomes an ideological ploy, providing the government with an excuse for its failure to secure certain human rights, such as the right to work, but the rule of law and the traditional freedom rights are not violated.

When the market functions well, in the sense that the result is economic growth, a government will want the credit for its success. However, even in such a situation legislators are reluctant to assume responsibility for the methods by which growth is furthered. There seems to exist some profound inconsistency between the techniques of legislation and law enforcement on the one hand, and the creation of new products, new behaviour, and new social forms on the other. Legal techniques, by contrast with ideal law, are geared to control and not to creation, yet there is no denying, as Hart and Hurst have claimed, that law in its traditional forms facilitates constructive action and paves the way for innovation.[13] Legal techniques are, however, ill suited to prescribing the steps by which a new and well defined state of affairs is to be achieved.

Outcomes of creative activity ('decisions' would be too ambitious a term) are determined by an appeal either to probable empirical truth or to worldly success. Through scientific discoveries and their utilization innovations are achieved. In chapter 4 it was shown that the legal mode of thinking clashes with the scientific one based upon notions of cause and effect or ends and means. Chapters 2 and 3 offered some reasons why legal technique had come to assume those characteristics that distinguish it from the causal-scientific model. In the market outcomes are frequently determined by the application of scientific methods, by research and development. But success is dependent upon competition, the outcome of which is only marginally predictable by scientific methods; it is to a large extent a question of trial and error within a very complicated maze of behaviour alternatives. This raises the question of whether it would be possible to institute competition by law and, through legal techniques to reward the winners.

Exemplary legal rewards

On theoretical grounds one would reject this as a viable method in a society that is dedicated to the rule of law while simultaneously accepting a market ideology. What the law can do, and actually does, is to establish and enforce the constituent rules of the game, including tampering with the conditions of competition. However, laws very rarely offer prizes to those who perform best in a competition to further some legally prescribed goal. To organize competition is to introduce uncertainty. There is no predictable relationship between an absolute level of performance and a set reward. All is relative; outcomes are determined by the performance of others.

When laws hold out rewards to citizens, these are usually linked to performance circumscribed in absolute terms, independent of how others might perform. If scarcity should force selection upon the distributing agency (e.g. a public bank), queuing or random devices may be used to choose the lucky ones. This means that the rewards are not exemplary, as penalties are.[14] The principles of sanction economy do not, apparently, operate positively. The law cannot reward a few in order to encourage the many. The stick may be applied to one delinquent in order to deter others from breaking the law, but there seem to be serious problems with using the carrot in the same way. The market, of course, is different. Many are spurred on by their observation of the few who win the big prizes. But then legal agencies do not serve as umpires in these contests. The law has transcended the morality of obligation through its ability to reward desirable behaviour, but it has not instituted a morality of excellence, if excellence means outstanding innovations and unusual performance.

This theoretically grounded hypothesis about the limitations of legal technique is supported by a review of Norwegian legislation covering the areas in which one might suspect that exemplary rewards or some reliance upon competition could be used as means of determining the distribution of awards. Very few instances can be found of the law's instituting some kind of competition, even a tacit one, for a prize to be distributed by a public agency.

Although not formally organized as a competition, the awarding of honours may serve as a system of exemplary rewards, combining support for excellence with the principle of sanction economy. According to the Norwegian Constitution (§23), it is the prerogative of the King (personally) to award medals, although it is stated explicitly that no further privileges are attached to the conferring of honours. In practice, no legal remedies are available to those who feel that they have been overlooked. Complaints would be considered bad form — an expression of snobbery or an overblown ego, maybe even as an insult to the King. The institution falls, as the market does, outside the area in which the rule of law and legal techniques are considered applicable. A reform-oriented government cannot use it to further specific programmes. The medals go, with few exceptions, to those who are already amply rewarded by success in the market or by high office. Here one might truly say, with Oscar Wilde, that nothing succeeds like success.[15]

The closest one can get to a positive parallel to the deterrent use of exemplary penalties is probably the institution of premium bonds. Many are encouraged to save by investing in these bonds, attracted by the chance of winning a prize. Sanction economy may operate here, but because of the guaranteed randomness of the selection of winners, there is neither competition nor reward for excellence. Similar considerations apply to other kinds of legally regulated lottery. Against the results of the random selection procedures losers have no legal redress. The rule of law demands no more than that the procedures should be random, guaranteeing everyone an equal chance to win.

One might expect that laws concerned with innovative endeavours, as in science and the arts, might exhibit instances of exemplary rewards and a morality of excellence. Perhaps the honorary degrees awarded by universities function in this way. Much the same could be said about them as about the honours awarded by a monarch. They provoke no issues that are amenable to legal techniques. In both cases one reason for this may be that arbitrarily administered success is more acceptable than arbitrary distributions at lower levels. By definition, not everyone can reach the top, while everyone can aim to avoid being punished or to gain access to generally available resources.

Patent law is directly concerned with innovation, rewarding inventors with monopoly rights to exploit their inventions. When the legal protection of inventions was discussed in England in the middle of the last century, there were those who advocated a system of publicly financed remuneration for inventors.[16] This was rejected in favour of the system that still exists in England and in other countries with a market economy, that of establishing monopoly rights and leaving it to the market to decide upon remuneration. The protection of inventors' rights is couched in traditional legal forms by prohibiting infringements of the patent rights. While the aim may be to encourage excellence in performance, again under competitive conditions, the legal techniques conform to a morality of obligation, which means preventing others from violating their duty not to interfere. Laws regulating prospecting and drilling for oil and gas, and their exploitations follow a similar pattern.

In the Soviet Union the legal situation is different. The state offers prizes to inventors, calculated on the basis of the cost savings that result from the introduction of new devices.[17] Labour law likewise offers a variety of prizes to those who excel in ability, diligence or loyalty. The inducements range from honorary citations and medals to tangible benefits like a holiday at the Black Sea, priority in housing or better educational opportunities for the children.[18] One gains the general impression that the award of medals and prizes in order to encourage excellence is a ubiquitous feature of the Soviet system, and in important areas it is authorized by legal enactment.

One reason for this deviation from the systems practised in Western Europe must be the massive extension of the public sphere in the Soviet Union and the consequently limited scope of the market. There seem to be strong social forces, irrespective of the political and economic system, that produce mechanisms, which can be public or private, that encourage excellence even if not always of exactly the same kind.

The difference is probably also related to the differences in conceptions of the rule of law (or socialist legality) and of the state that have already been mentioned (pp. 42 and 157). In principle, there is consensus in a communist nation about the direction in which excellence lies. There is an all encompassing theory about the good society and the good citizen from which one may derive criteria for measuring excellence. In the Western world a similar assumption prevails within the scientific field. In other arenas, however, it is commonly assumed that a plurality of goals and values must coexist peacefully (see p. 50); whatever consensus there may be, it primarily concerns minimum standards of conduct.

In so far as Western legal systems promote new types of behaviour or encourage the pursuit of excellence, they do not seem to do so by means of exemplary rewards. Two important exceptions are perhaps the use of grades in the educational system and the competition for positions in the Civil Service. Competitive grade systems have frequently been set up by prescribing a normal distribution of grades: 20 per cent high grades, 60 per cent medium grades and 20 per cent low grades. This means that the fate of the individual pupil will depend on competition within the universe of pupils to which this normal distribution is applicable. Although the normal distribution pattern seems to have been imposed in a very liberal way, the grade and examination system provides exemplary rewards for those who excel, although it tends simultaneously to weed out under-achievers, the school losers, often with dire consequences for their future career and destiny.

The grade system in Norwegian schools, at all levels, has become a highly controversial matter and a central political issue. It touches upon sensitive values like social equality and the importance of achievement, often with contradictory implications. Policies vacillate, while the question of evaluation is under apparently interminable scrutiny by government committees. However, questions related to the rule of law have played a minor role in these debates. It is only recently that grading and examinations have been viewed as reflecting decisions that might be open to judicial review or to quasi-legal remedies.

There are many reasons for this neglect of the legal issues involved in the assessment of educational achievement. Only recently has educational achievement extensively supplanted or supplemented birth and market forces as determinants of an individual's class position and his access to resources. As with medical decisions (albeit not to the same degree), the assessment of achievement in school has been seen as a professional matter, a task for which teachers alone have the expertise. There is, in principle, a unitary standard for assessing the degree to which a person has acquired knowledge.

In any event, the grade and examination system deviates significantly from other kinds of exemplary reward with respect to the parsimony of sanctions. If we regard schooling as a contest between recruits to the different social strata, it costs the public a great deal to keep this contest going, comprising as it does approximately one-third of the population. It should also be emphasized that the grades themselves are mere symbols. What they mean in practice is decided by others, increasingly the state in its role as employer.

Education and science have a logic of their own. This logic is at variance with the traditional logic of the law as we have tried to outline it in preceding chapters. New legal techniques may emerge as instruments to deal with the intrinsic requirements of science and education, so that the educational institutions will better meet those fundamental human needs to which the law has served as a response.

The challenge of human rights

It seems clear then, from the analyses offered above that legal personnel of all sorts face formidable challenges today and will even more in the near future. It has become apparent that in the welfare states legislation as much as legal practice is shot through with contradictions and tensions. The problems would have loomed even larger had this book dealt also with international law and with countries in which other legal systems prevail. Our perspective has been a narrower one, yet it presents a perplexing array of unsolved — perhaps insoluble — problems.

We discern that there is a trend to legislate for new human rights of the social and cultural kind and to attempt to make them justiciable. The traditional 'freedom rights' continue to be upheld, based, as before, upon distrust of the government and the state. Herein lies a basic problem because governments are becoming increasingly dependent upon the citizens in their effort to secure that level of prosperity which is a precondition for the fulfilment of the promises held out in enactments on social and cultural rights.

This is the great difference between the old and the new human rights: the 'freedom rights' impose negative obligations upon the government, the obligation not to interfere with the activities of the citizens unless authorized to do so through the due process of law. True, it has sometimes been difficult for a government to abide by this obligation in periods of crises when economic or other hardship has threatened the very foundation on which the leadership has built its legitimacy. But governments that are dedicated, by law and electoral promise, to the realization of the new human rights face the resource problem more or less continuously.[19]

The dilemma has surfaced, for example, in this form. Access to adequate health care is a human right in a welfare state and is based on legislative enactments. Although the justiciability of this right is limited, a government will be under strong pressure to act if there is a serious failure of the health system. One cause of failure may be the geographically or socially skewed distribution of doctors or dentists; a remedial act might be to introduce compulsory service for doctors in medically backward areas. However, doctors who have been ordered to serve under such schemes have felt this to be an infringement of their professional 'freedom rights'. Some such cases have ended up in the European Court of Human Rights.

Although such cases may be exceptional, the underlying problems are endemic. In chapter 5 the problem was raised of how the *right* to work could be made effective without simultaneously introducing a *duty* to work. The dilemma can be generalized: how can a right to consume be sustained without a corresponding duty to produce? Within the market this correspondence prevails. The problem arises today because of the uneasy intersection of the market and the public sphere, often in the form of a question: who belongs where?

There was a time, in the heyday of liberal ideology, when the relationship between consumption and production was linked very closely with the individual. This was not merely the concomitant of entrepreneurship in trade and industry; it was also an implicit element in the ethos of subsistence farming. In spite of the strong individualist and liberal trends in current legal policy in the Western world, a collectivist image of the relationship between consumption and production is being portrayed by politicians, civil servants and the mass media. The task is formulated as one of securing a sufficiently high national product to pay for social services and the various other schemes that are aimed at improving living conditions for everybody.

The combination of this collectivist image of progress with the individualistic models underlying the human rights approach (as interpreted within the traditional legal mould) may induce serious strains in the social fabric. Although problems of the legitimacy of the state may arise, the most important conflicts need not be those between the citizens and the state apparatus. Nor is it likely that the traditional class conflicts centred on the antagonistic interests of capital and labour will play as large a part as they have done in the recent past. New and different lines of cleavage are emerging, often in the form of a clash of interests between those who are assumed to be the producers and those who are assumed to be consumers but who do not contribute their share to the national product.

The legal model, centred on individualized subjects, presumes that it is possible to distinguish clearly between give and take, between cost and benefit, between a right and a duty. Increasingly, these contrasts are being blurred. Conceptions of justice presuppose some kind of weighing on a scale. Criteria of measurement are needed – above all consensual criteria. Today there is often doubt. Where formerly there was agreement that more products and a higher level of consumption was desirable, and disagreement focused mainly on the distribution of wealth, now there are doubts in many areas about the desirability of further growth. When does more health care and more advanced medicine turn into a menace? When does the further reduction of work hours and the lowering of the age of retirement become a threat to the individual's meaningful existence?

These are problems for the legislator, preferably aided by two mechanisms – a more effective system of public participation, and the findings of the social sciences. The two sources will often provide law-makers with contradictory clues, leaving them with a delicate task that demands a certain understanding of the social sciences. When basic societal goals are controversial, a refinement of the participatory rights of the citizen is much needed. The traditional notion of 'one man one vote' will not do in the many areas in which interest in outcomes is very unevenly distributed among the electorate, so that some have a life-long attachment to the issues at stake while others come and go. The law of the future will have to work towards a representative system, in private organizations as well, that is better adapted to the interests and attachments of the members.[20] The human right upon which such endeavours are founded is the right to participate, the right to influence or produce outcomes and not merely to receive the fruits of a more or less democratic process of decision-making.

There will always be flaws in representative systems, threats to minorities, over-exposure to demagogic and partisan propaganda and so on. Corrective mechanisms are needed, and the social sciences may provide some. Through their ability to reveal the tacit and the latent as well as possible future implications or consequences, they lend a voice, however feeble, to interests that would otherwise go unnoticed or remain too muted to gain recognition. Not least important, the sociology of law might contribute to a realistic understanding of how the increasing demand for justice can be met by introducing those quantitative factors, time and money, that determine access to the law.

This book has dealt with forms rather than with substance, with procedures rather than with the goals that these procedures serve. We have been concerned with the gap between two modes of thinking: one in terms of cause and effect, and one in terms of justice, the latter built upon a comparison of achievements and of sanctions, positive and negative. The analysis has not, however, delved into the problem of which causes, which effects, which achievements, which sanctions. This may need a few words of justification.

History is shaped more by forces than by decisions. It is a succession of events rather than the unfolding of human plans. Individual choices aggregate in unforeseen patterns. While that is so, all attempts to modify social development, to prevent social ills, to further human well-being by conscious collective action must take place formally. Methods must be chosen. I hope that this book may contribute to an understanding of what legal methods are, to what purposes they may be applied and, not least, where they will fail unless they are modified or supplemented by other instruments of governance and conflict resolution.

Finally, it should be recognized that substance and form intersect. When problems are institutionalized as legal issues, this has an impact upon public opinion. With the vast increase in the level of education and the penetration of the mass media, this impact is gaining in strength just as public opinion has become a social force of great potential. How people think about political, economic, social and religious issues is more than a question of form. It has become a driving force in history.

Notes

1 Cf. Marc Galanter, 'The modernization of law', in Lawrence M. Friedman and Stuart Macauly, *Law and the Behavioral Sciences* (Indianapolis/New York: Bobbs-Merrill, 1977), pp. 1046–55.
2 See Maurice Cranston, *What are Human Rights?* (London/Sydney/Toronto, The Bodley Head, 1973), p. 7.
3 Wesley Newcomb Hohfeld, *Fundamental Legal Conceptions* (New Haven; Yale University Press, 1923). See also John P. Plamenatz, *Consent, Freedom and Political Obligation* (London/Oxford/New York: Oxford University Press, 1968), pp. 82ff.
4 C. B. Macpherson, *The Political Theory of Possessive Individualism.* (Oxford: Clarendon Press, 1962).
5 Jan F. Triska, *Constitutions of the Communist Party-States* (Stanford: Stanford University Press, 1968). See also Cranston, *What are Human Rights?,* pp. 65ff.; Arthur Henry Robertson, *Human Rights in the World* (Manchester, Manchester University Press, 1972), esp. pp. 38ff. On international agreements, see Walter Laqueur and Barry Rubin (eds.), *The Human Rights Reader* (New York/Scarborough, Ont.: New American Library, 1977), pp. 193–263.
6 Asa Briggs, 'The welfare state in historical perspective', *Archives Européennes de Sociologie,* 2 (1961), p. 228.
7 See *Socialist Concept of Human Rights* (Budapest: Akadémiai Kiadó, 1966), pp. 57–9.
8 Cf. James Willard Hurst, *Law and Social Progress in United States History* (Ann Arbor: University of Michigan Press, 1960), pp. 99ff. H. L. A. Hart, *The Concept of Law* (Oxford: Oxford University Press, 1961), p. 27.
9 Cf. Ernest Gellner, *Thought and Change* (Chicago: University of Chicago Press, 1965), p. 33.
10 Karl Olivecrona, *Rättsordningen. Idéer och Fakta* (The Legal Order: Ideas and Facts) (Lund: C. W. K. Gleerūp, 1966), p. 265.
11 See above, p. 9.
12 Michel Crozier, Samuel P. Huntington and Joji Watanuki, *The Crisis of Democracy* (New York: New York University Press, 1975, p. 159).
13 Cf. note 8.
14 For a brief but illuminating note on the asymmetry between penalties and rewards, see Friedman and Macauly, *Law and the Behavioral Sciences,* pp. 341–2.
15 Originally from Alexandre Dumas, Sr, *Ange Pitou* (Paris: 1854).
16 J. W. Baxter, *World Patent Law and Practice* (London: Sweet & Maxwell/New York: Matthew Bender, 1973), pp. 14ff.
17 John N. Hazard, *Communists and Their Law. A Search for the Common Core of the Legal Systems of the Marxian Socialist States* (Chicago/London: University of Chicago Press, 1969), pp. 243ff., esp. pp. 251–3.
18 *Gazette of the Supreme Soviet of the USSR,* 29 (1970), item 285.
19 It seems that it is this difference that leads Cranston to reject economic, social and cultural rights as human rights: *What are Human Rights?,* pp. 65ff.
20 Cf. James Coleman, 'Political Money', *American Political Science Review,* 64 (1970), pp. 1074–87. See also Gunther Teubner, *Organisationsdemokratie un Verbandsverfassung* (Tübingen: J. C. B. Mohr (Paul Siebeck), 1978).

Select bibliography

Aubert, Vilhelm, (ed.), *Sociology of Law* (Harmondsworth: Penguin, 1969)

Black, Donald, *The Behavior of Law* (New York: Academic Press, 1976)

Campbell, Colin, and Wiles, Paul (eds.), *Law and Society* (Oxford: Martin Robertson, 1979)

Eckhoff, Torstein, *Justice: its Determinants in Social Interaction* (Rotterdam: Rotterdam University Press, 1974)

Ehrlich, Eugen, *Fundamental Principles of the Sociology of Law* (New York: Russell & Russell, 1962)

d'Entrèvres, A. P., *Natural Law,* 2nd edn. (London: Hutchinson, 1979)

Friedman, Lawrence M., and Macauly, Stuart, *Law and the Behavioral Sciences,* 2nd edn. (Indianapolis/New York: Bobbs-Merrill, 1977)

Friedmann, Wolfgang, *Legal Theory,* 5th edn. (London: Stevens & Sons, 1967)

Fuller, Lon L., *The Morality of Law* (New Haven/London: Yale University Press, 1964)

Gluckman, Max, *The Judicial Process among the Barotse of Northern Rhodesia* (Manchester: Manchester University Press, 1955)

Hart, H. L. A., *The Concept of Law* (Oxford: Oxford University Press, 1961)

Hogarth, John, *Sentencing as a Human Process* (Toronto: University of Toronto Press, 1971)

Hoebel, E. Adamson, *The Law of Primitive Man* (Cambridge, Mass.: Harvard University Press, 1954)

Hurst, James Willard, *Law and Social Process in United States History* (Ann Arbor: University of Michigan Press, 1960)

Kalven, Harry, Jr, and Zeisel, Hans, *The American Jury* (Boston/Toronto: Little, 1966)

Nader, Laura (ed.), *Law in Culture and Society* (Chicago: Aldine, 1969)

Nader, Laura, and Todd, Harvey F. (eds.), *The Disputing Process – Law in Ten Societies* (New York: Columbia University Press, 1978)

Podgórecki, Adam, *Law and Society* (London: Routledge and Kegan Paul, 1974)

Renner, Karl, *The Institutions of Private Law and their Social Functions* (London: Routledge & Kegan Paul, 1949)

Robertson, Arthur Henry, *Human Rights in the World* (Manchester: Manchester University Press, 1972)

Ross, Alf, *On Law and Justice* (London: Stevens & Sons, 1958)

Schubert, Glendon (ed.), *Judicial Decision-Making* (Glencoe, III.: Free Press, 1963)

Selznick, Philip, *et al., Law, Society and Industrial Justice* (New York: Russell Sage Foundation, 1969)

Twining, William, *Karl Llewellyn and the Realist Movement* (London: Weidenfeld & Nicolson, 1973)

Index